D1497817

REFLECTIONS ON THE GOSPELS

REFLECTIONS ON
THE GOSPELS

By

J. W. C. WAND, D.D.
Treasurer of St. Paul's; formerly Bishop of London

LONDON
A. R. MOWBRAY & CO LTD

© A. R. Mowbray & Co Ltd 1969

Printed in Great Britain by
Alden & Mowbray Ltd
at the Alden Press, Oxford

SBN 264 65572 9

First published in 1969

To A. E.
who made the first selection

PREFACE

THIS volume completes the trilogy on the collects, epistles and gospels of the Church's year. Like the previous volumes it comprises articles published over the last decade in the *Church Times*, and I am grateful to the proprietors and editor of that periodical for permission to reproduce them here.

It will be noticed that normally the reflections take the form of expositions of the biblical text. Very occasionally, however, there has been a change of style when the gospel of the day does not seem clearly to reflect the subject of the liturgical season.

I am glad to take this opportunity of thanking readers, both clerical and lay, who have kindly written to me about the previous volumes and about the articles as they have appeared week by week in the press.

✠ WM. WAND

1968

CONTENTS

REFLECTIONS ON THE GOSPELS

REFLECTIONS ON
THE GOSPELS

COMING IN GLORY

THE gaze of the infant Church was fixed upon the Lord's return in majesty. They had seen so much of his humiliation.

What more appropriate than his return in glory, when every eye should see him, when his cause would be proclaimed triumphant, and when he would be recognized as ruler over all the earth? It was the contemplation of such a future that kept at bay every despondent thought and maintained alive a vigorous, creative hope.

Such thoughts were all the easier because, if Jesus was what he was claimed to be, glory was his natural condition. It was almost a physical thing. It was the *Shekinah*, the luminous cloud in which Jehovah had descended to lead the children of Israel through the wilderness, and in which he had rested over the tabernacle. That Jesus had shared it had been made clear to chosen representatives at the Transfiguration, and also at the Ascension. Surely, then, it would be with the same glory of his Father that he would appear again from heaven with all the company of the angelic host.

*   *   *

Such would be the ultimate revelation, the final unveiling of his character as Victor, Saviour and Judge.

Then it would be made clear that what he had taught and suffered for was the truth. The secret of existence was not to be found in material wealth and power or position. The secret of God was with those who were meek and lowly of heart, who were prepared to give and serve even if they received no recognition.

This truth, thus finally revealed and vindicated, would be the goal of history. It has recently been said by a great commentator that there is no goal to history. But that is a hard saying. It is essential to the Christian dispensation that history should issue in something. The idea that the course of events goes round in circles, or that it is entirely shapeless is utterly pagan. For the Christian there has always been a great, far-off, divine event, to which the whole creation moves, although he has not always been certain about the epithet 'far-off'.

But whether sooner or later, whether in time or eternity, whether in history or outside, there is an end which shall also be a beginning. That is the essential meaning of Advent. And because we believe that God is good, we believe that the end will also be good, and that he will come no longer in humiliation but in majesty.

*   *   *

That conviction does not conceal from us the fact that the Coming, when it occurs, will be for judgment. That is why we are given in the gospel for today the story of the cleansing of the temple. When God comes to his own, it is inevitable that evil will be revealed for what it is. By the side of his utter whiteness, every other shade from grey to black will be quite obvious. That is the necessary effect of light: it must show the true character of what it reveals.

In this case the standard is a moral one. The issue by which the world will be judged is the distinction between right and wrong, between good and evil. The Advent makes it clear that this is the only measuring-rod, the one standard by which we must judge all our 'differentials'.

*   *   *

This, then, unlocks the secret of the universe; it gives us the clue to existence; it tells us what we are here for; it reveals the meaning and purpose of history. You and I have come into this world to be prepared for eternity. God has stored up for us an everlasting bliss at whose true nature we can hardly guess. But we do know that we could not adequately appreciate it unless we were like him.

And so we are here to be made like him and we can only be made like him as we learn to imitate his character of goodness. Hence the long-drawn struggle in which we take our part. It is the school in which we learn. Advent is pictured as the dramatic moment at which school ends, the meaning of it is made clear, and we enter into the larger life of glory for which it has been our preparation.

THE WORD

BIBLE Sunday is a characteristically Anglican institution. It will always have a great appeal for us, for
there is no church that makes so extended a use of the
Bible in public worship.

Apart from the monthly recitation of the Psalter, the
daily office imposes four lessons upon us every day of the
week, and in churches with a daily Eucharist an epistle
and gospel are also read. Six sizeable lections a day are
good evidence of the practical reverence we pay the
scriptures. Through all the revisions of the lectionary
we still maintain the rough and ready rule of reading
the Old Testament once each year and the New Testament twice.

*   *   *

Of the importance we attach to the scriptures thus
frequently read, our Articles leave us in no doubt. They
seem to stretch themselves to the utmost to put the Bible
above both Church and Councils. While there is no
attempt to disguise the fact that the Church gave us the
scriptures, it is clearly held that the canon sealed the
tradition, and that henceforth nothing can be imposed as
an article of faith that cannot be proved directly from the
scriptures. The Old Testament Apocrypha, representing
the excess of the Greek or Alexandrian canon over the
Hebrew or Palestinian canon, is still retained for public
reading, but its authority is limited to edification, and
it is not used for the formulation of doctrine.

It is in accord with this exalted view that the priest
at his ordination is solemnly presented with a copy of the

scriptures and given authority to preach the Word of God. Henceforth, we speak of his ministry as that of the Word and Sacraments, putting the Word first in its logical order, as God's self-revelation comes before his redemptive work, and faith comes before practice.

*   *   *

In what sense is the Bible the Word of God? A word is a means of communication. The Word of God is the instrument by which God holds communion with men: it is the agent by which he reveals himself to men. But God, it may be said, did not actually write the Bible: it did not come to us, already printed or written, from heaven. Surely we know that the list of books we now have between the covers of our Bible was not apparently fixed till well into the fourth century A.D.

We know, too, that each one of the component books has a considerable history behind it, and that often it is itself a composition of several earlier documents. In what sense can such an anthology, which has gone through many changes of so long a literary history, be God's Word to us?

Well, we can say in the first place that God's revelation is of himself as a person, and that a person is revealed mostly in what he does. The Bible is the record of God's mighty acts leading up to his visible entry into the sphere of time and space in the person of his Son, and thus establishing his Church among men. God inspired chosen men to recognize those mighty acts for what they were, and to record them for the benefit of others.

Similarly, men were inspired to record or explain the life, teaching and work of Christ. Thus the Bible is much more than a history of Israel; it is more even than a record of the mighty acts of God worked out in that history; it is a revelation of the character and purpose of God as

B

manifested in those mighty acts. It is true that this revelation comes to a head in the Incarnation and in the ministry of Jesus Christ who was himself in a special sense the Word or utterance of God, but inasmuch as the whole record leads up to or derives from him, it too shares in his title as Word of God.

*　　　*　　　*

The practical question for us is how we are to read this Word so that we can gain the utmost benefit from it. The answer is threefold: First, in the literal sense, bringing to it all the best information we can gain on its composition and background so that we can understand it as a piece of literature.

Second, in the moral sense, distinguishing 'what became divine guidance in the Hebrews' experience so that it may become divine guidance for us'. And third, in the spiritual sense, so immersing ourselves in the mood of what is written that through it God may speak directly to our own souls. Then, and not till then, does the Bible become fully for us the Word of God. And his word shall not pass away.

THE MINISTRY

AFTER the Bible comes the ministry. Advent III is as closely associated with the thoughts of the sacred ministry as is Advent II with that of the Word. It is well that it should be so, for it is clear that in the scriptures themselves great attention is paid to the nature and work of the ministry, and it is definitely stated to be one of Christ's gifts to men. We ought not then to regard the clergy as just another professional class like lawyers, doctors or teachers (although we should always desire them to pursue the ideals of professional excellence), but we should think of them as God's messengers and ministrants, and try to trust them as such.

The foundation of the ministry is laid in the person of Christ himself. He, as St. Peter says in his first Epistle, is the Shepherd and Bishop of our souls. How he ministered on behalf of his Father to human individuals is set out in every line of the Gospels. We are to do the same. 'As my Father hath sent me, even so send I you.' We do then still today actually share in his ministry.

*   *   *

The work of the ministers is divided into two parts: the pastoral and the evangelistic.

The first implies careful attendance upon the flock committed to them. There have been times and places in which this seemed the total duty. The pastor had his parish, and practically everyone in it looked to him as the person responsible for their souls. Something like that must have been the position of George Herbert in the village of Bemerton. Indeed some of us can still look back to the time when it seemed natural for a parish priest to think of his parish and his congregation as practically identical.

It will always remain true that the clergy will bear a special responsibility for the flock who acknowledge them, just as Jesus felt a special regard for his own followers. 'Fear not, little flock, it is your Father's good pleasure to give you the Kingdom.'

It is a pity that even regular Church-people are not always ready to use the good offices of their clergy. After all the priest is (or should be) the friend of everyone without exception. But outsiders are hardly likely to come to him unless they see his own people seeking his help.

*   *   *

While this pastoral aspect of the ministry still persists, and is indeed as necessary as ever, we are being compelled today to recognize the primary importance of evangelization. The proportion between the congregation in church and the population outside has altered. We have not only a large body of non-practising Christians but a growing body of essential pagans. In such a situation it is more clearly evident than ever how important it is to go out and seek and to save the sheep that is lost.

It needs a new kind of ministry, outward, rather than inward, looking. It means trying one method after another of reaching the unchurched multitudes, until at last some sort of success is gained. It means above all enlisting the laity, and inducing them to see that they occupy a foremost place in this ministry. What the preacher must do in the pulpit, they can do in the home, in the office, on the farm, at the assembly-line—not by actual preaching but by allowing their lives to witness to their faith and by openly acknowledging that faith when occasion calls.

We shall not waste time asking who is to blame for the present desertion of Christ. The Church has always made her witness; and we have never been led to expect an easy victory. We must bear our own share of responsibility while refusing to sentimentalize over those who deliberately stop their ears.

In any case it is God's battle, and if we are faithful he will give to his ministers, whether clergy or laity, the success he desires.

VOICE IN THE WILDERNESS

IT is extraordinary how in the course of ages, words and phrases change their meaning. Today, the description, 'a voice in the wilderness' is a declaration of despair. It suggests a solitary person demanding the redress of some great wrong, or the satisfaction of some dire need, and receiving no attention whatsoever. To us, the phrase carries with it as an undertone, either the macabre satisfaction of the self-designated martyr, or the grim depression of one who finds himself without sympathy and without friends.

How different was the phrase in its first meaning. It was then no forlorn hope, but a shout of triumph. It heralded the imminent return of the Jews from their long exile in Babylon. It was a challenge to all and sundry to set to work to prepare their way. A road must be built straight across the desert, so that they need not go all the way round the Fertile Crescent. Every valley must be filled in, and every mountain and hill must be laid low.

You would have thought that in that sixth century B.C. they were going to build one of our most modern motor highways.

*   *   *

The cry still carried its note of triumph and of challenge to the ears of the earliest Christians. It announced the imminent arrival of Messiah to lead his people out of their old-world captivity into the New Age. They associated the voice with John the Baptist, the forerunner, who challenged people to prepare the way for the New Age by changing their lives, and so inaugurated the last great reform movement in Judaism.

It was a long time since the moral note had been so forcibly struck. Men had often been encouraged to take up arms and shed blood to make a way for the coming King, but to be called upon to repent and be baptized was new to their generation.

John's insistence was a great help to the first Christian generation. Otherwise their task was difficult enough. To persuade their contemporaries that the New Age had arrived, that the return to Paradise, to the conditions of the garden of Eden, had actually begun: this was not easy at a time when they were feeling the weight of Jewish opposition and were still under Roman dominance.

Their task was made still harder by the fact that their Messiah had come and gone, had been condemned as a criminal by Roman and Jew alike, and for his alleged crimes had actually been executed upon the Cross. How could they repeat the cry of triumph and challenge people to keep on the tip-toe of expectation for his return in glory?

*   *   *

Yet that is what they did. They drew a distinction between the two Advents. They recognized that they were living between the first Christmas and the Last Judgment. They lived in a perpetual tension between the 'already' and the 'not yet'. Their challenge lost a little of its triumphant quality and took on a new urgency of repentance, though it was long before it acquired the quality of 'fear and trembling' that Kierkegaard thought to be its due, and longer still before the Voice was regarded as that of one doomed to neglect and consequent despair. Still the paradox was there, 'Rejoice in the Lord alway' and 'Pass your time of sojourning here in fear.'

Today we stand at the very centre of that paradox as we keep the last Sunday of Advent and prepare for the

Christmas feast. We remember that the only true way to complete joy is through penitential fear. We can confess our sins and so make a way for Messiah's coming in our hearts. We can prepare our crib and make sure that the New Age of his Kingdom is established in our home.

Then when Christmas comes there will be no longer room for any kind of dread, but only for that perfect love that casteth out fear. The Voice will ring out once more with its old triumphant note, and we shall know that in our own little corner of the world at least, the task of preparing a highway for our God is well under way.

INCARNATION

WHAT was the character and purpose of the Incarnation? Literally the word means 'entering into flesh'. But obviously such a definition is not nearly large enough to contain the mystery of our redemption. To understand the character of the Incarnation we can begin where St. John does in the prologue to the Fourth Gospel, that is, in the eternal sphere where God's thought expresses itself in a Word. This Word gave the directions by which at the beginning of time the material universe was made. Now, in these latter days, says St. John, it has spoken again and has been embodied in human nature.

This is the meaning of what happened at Bethlehem. Men had been looking for some heaven-sent messenger to deliver them from their wrongs. And now he came, to their utter surprise, not on the morning clouds of majesty, nor with the rolling drums of a conqueror, but in a 'little baby thing that made a woman cry'.

*   *   *

If we go on to ask the purpose of this Incarnation, we find that it is twofold: first for revelation and then for redemption.

First, the heavenly Child, as he grows up and lives the life of man among men, reveals the nature of God, as it had never been fully revealed before. No doubt prophets and lawgivers and wise men had had much to say about the character of God, and those who were willing to listen had learned much about him. But now he was revealed to men as one of themselves in terms that they could better understand. Here was no pulpit exhortation or

professor's lecture, but man living the normal life of a
man among men. It was God expressing himself as fully
as possible in the terms of human nature. Men saw the
glory of God revealed in the face of Jesus Christ.

But Jesus revealed even more than that. He showed
the goodness that is possible for men when they yield
themselves completely to God's power and guidance.

Also the Incarnation made clear the true nature of the
universe. The environment in which we live is not some
alien sphere entirely cut off from God. As in Christ the
eternal Word inhabits human flesh, so God lives in and
through his material world. He is not far removed from
any one of us. 'Earth's crammed with Heaven and every
common bush afire with God.' The Incarnation makes
clear the sacramental nature of the whole universe.

*   *   *

The purpose of the Incarnation was not only revelation
but also redemption. Jesus came to redeem his people
from their sins. Sin was a legacy inherited by all the human
race and every individual within it. But Christ came, the
one perfect Man, and broke the entail of sin.

The way of escape was, and is, through union with
Christ. If we are joined with him we have become fellow-
heirs with him of a different kind of legacy, that of eternal
life, which begins here and now. If we are made one with
him we have entered upon an entirely new type of life
with new powers, new possibilities, new responsibilities.

Jesus set a fresh standard; that of perfection. We should
never have dreamt it possible to reach that standard, if he
had not actually done so in the terms of our human life.
Even now we can only regard it in our own case as a
potentiality, something that can only happen if the
conditions are right.

Here our Christmas communion comes to our aid. In

it our individual personality assimilates the person of Christ, just as our physical body assimilates the elements of bread and wine. Here is the true issue of the Incarnation for us—the eternal Word of God, born in a manger, and now born again in our hearts. It is in our unity with him that all he has revealed of God and his ways comes alive.

THE BIRTH OF JESUS

IT is possible to see a double intention in St. Matthew's narrative of the birth of Jesus.

He wishes to fix in his readers' minds the precise details of the miracle. And he wishes to assure them that this was truly the beginning of a new era, the era in which they themselves were privileged to live. So he is careful to let them see that this is his own special account, and that the birth of Jesus Christ was precisely 'on this wise'.

It was important for them to recognize that the whole action was due to the operation of the Holy Spirit. He who had been the agent in the creation of the whole world exercised his special function in the case of the Virgin Mary. The power that had caused the world to be born was responsible for the promise of a new birth through her.

We must remember that St. Matthew's readers believed themselves to be living under a special dispensation of the Spirit's influence. All alike were encouraged, as we still are, to perceive the Spirit's working in their own personality. They would find a particular proof of it in the special and unique happening in the case of the Blessed Virgin.

Of all people the one who had the greatest reason to doubt was Joseph. But he was a good man and God would not let him go wrong. And so the truth of what had happened was validated for him in a dream.

*   *   *

Matthew, however, is not content with signs and portents. He wants to show that this miraculous birth is entirely in line with the customary action of God. There comes to his mind a passage of Isaiah, in which the prophet uses the incidence of a birth (possibly in the royal family) to assure his people that a new and happier epoch is about to begin in their history.

The passage was all the more appropriate for Matthew's use inasmuch as the Greek translation had described the mother as a virgin. In course of time the prophecy had been associated with the coming of the Messiah, and this made it all the more telling.

The suggestion was further strengthened by the name that was to be given to the child. 'Emmanuel' meant 'God with us', and betokened the new confidence Israel was to feel in the guidance and protection of God. It would indeed be difficult to select a passage from the Old Testament more thoroughly appropriate to the circumstances of Christ's birth. It has been associated with the Christmas story ever since. As Matthew intended, it helps us to realize that God is the same yesterday, today, and for ever.

                    *   *   *

After the preliminaries and the quotation from the Old Testament the narrative moves swiftly and decisively to its conclusion. 'Then Joseph, being raised from sleep, did as the angel of the Lord had bidden him.' He protects his bride: the baby is born; and its name was called Jesus, 'Jehovah saves'.

It is St. Luke who tells us that the name was officially conferred upon the child at his circumcision eight days after birth, and who confirms that this was in fulfilment of the prediction of the angel who had announced the coming birth to Mary. The name is important, not only because it indicates the part that salvation is to play in Jesus' own life and work, but also because it indicates that the special period of salvation has begun.

It is in line with the name Emmanuel, God with us, reminding the reader of a time past when Jehovah had manifested his presence with his chosen people and had inaugurated a new period of prosperity for them. Today there was being inaugurated a new period not of material so much as of spiritual prosperity.

It is fitting that we should be reminded of this truth at the beginning of a new year.

Our difficulty is to keep the recognition of our enhanced opportunity vividly before our eyes. Why not make this New Year's Day a reflection, concentrated as in a mirror, of the new era won for us in Christ?

THE FULNESS OF CHRIST

Christmas II   *St. John* 1. 14

A STRANGE phrase—the fulness of Christ—and one
whose meaning at first sight is not at all obvious.
But it is important for us to know, for Sunday's gospel
says we have all received it, and it is foolish to remain
in the possession of gifts without knowing what they are.
Most of us have been made aware of that axiom this
Christmastide!

The word 'fulness' is often applied to the term Godhead, and is meant to suggest that God contains within
himself everything that is both good and powerful. Since
it is here applied to Jesus Christ, it is a tacit assertion of
the fact that Jesus shares in the full nature of the Godhead.
The New English Bible translates the passage, 'Out of his
full store we have all received grace upon grace', which
makes it a little easier for us to understand. But, inasmuch
as 'grace' and 'gift' are often the same word in Greek, the
translators might have carried through their own line of
thought more completely if they had said 'Out of his full
store we have all received gift after gift.'

In any case the sense is that Jesus contains in himself
all that is good, and out of his infinite treasure he has
bestowed upon us an incalculable wealth and variety of
free presents.

*   *   *

Two particular ingredients of this 'fulness' are chosen
out for special mention—grace and truth. Their copious
emergence with Christ was indeed epoch-making: it
started a new era in world-history. As the giving of the
Law through Moses had inaugurated one period, so

the distribution of grace and truth through Christ inaugurated another and greater dispensation. That this is truly so, subsequent generations have acknowledged by actually dividing the chronology of human history into two portions, B.C. and A.D., at the birth of Jesus.

At the first coming of Jesus the world received a fresh knowledge of truth. It was enlightened as to the nature of God, and his plan for the universe. This was the secret that the angels had long desired to look into but had not been able to penetrate.

This truth was not mere intellectual knowledge: it was accompanied by God's 'grace' or favour. That implied a power by which the new knowledge might be made effective. The new knowledge was not just to be known by the mind or repeated by the lips: it was meant to change the lives both of individuals and of nations.

*　　　*　　　*

It is odd that in these days we should be so afraid of recognizing the objectivity of this revelation. It seems to be felt as a necessary concession to science that we should conceive of God in the vaguest and least personal terms possible. But science itself is not at all vague. Its whole existence depends upon its capacity to deal with weights and measures in the most exact way conceivable. Nevertheless one suspects that, when the scientist gets away from his laboratory, he is only too glad to shed all that precision and to think again in human and personal terms.

So we know God as personal, because the only-begotten Son, which is in the bosom of the Father, has declared him so to be. Here the New English Bible translates beautifully, 'No one has ever seen God: but God's only Son, he who is nearest to the Father's heart, he has made him known.'

Could anything be more thoroughly personal? It is good that we should be reminded that God is 'in here' as well as 'out there', that he is 'the ground of our being' as well as the majestic ruler over earth and sky. But through all he is the Father as revealed by the Son. His grace is the loving influence he exercises over every one of his children, nourishing us in all goodness and happiness, and strengthening our character so that we may face undismayed the many changes and chances of this mortal life.

As we share the fulness of Christ we enter more fully into the Father's glory.

C

THE UNVEILING OF CHRIST

Epiphany *St. Matthew* 2. 1

THE placing of the Magi among the figures of the crib symbolizes the third chapter in the long story of the Incarnation. The first was the Annunciation, the second the Nativity, and now comes the Epiphany, which itself is described in three incidents.

The distinctive association of the manifestation or unveiling of Christ with the visit of the Wise Men from the East is a characteristic feature of our Western liturgical tradition. The mysterious East with all its traditional splendour and astrological learning represents the Gentile world that had had no share in God's special self-revelation. The Wise Men are not ashamed to come to the least of the cities of a despised nation to find a babe whose glorious destiny they had seen written in the skies.

The humility of the learned men matched the humble circumstances in which they found the Holy Family. T. S. Eliot depicts them long afterwards pondering over the mystery of it. Was it a birth or a death they had seen? Herod's slaughter or God's new beginning? At least God here reveals himself as dwelling with the humble and lowly of heart. He has come down a long way to meet our need.

* * *

Another incident in the story of Christ's manifestation is opened to us in the lection relating to his baptism. This was indeed the original element in the Epiphany observance, as it was inaugurated in the Eastern Church. The unique importance of Christ's baptism generally escapes the modern reader of the Bible. By way of contrast some

22

of the early heretics exaggerated it so much that they made it the very beginning, and indeed the source, of the Incarnation. The Greek Fathers struck the right balance in keeping the memorial of it as the great unveiling of Christ's true character to the world.

Here is revealed to us, as was perhaps revealed to Jesus himself, the true nature of the mission he had been sent to accomplish. Here he is made known as the Messiah who will save the world by suffering. The Synoptic Gospels tell us of the voice from heaven and the descent of the Holy Spirit, but as usual it is the Fourth Gospel that penetrates to the heart of the matter: 'Behold the Lamb of God that taketh away the sin of the world.'

It is not the humility of Jesus that is here in the foreground but his greatness, the stupendous nature of the apostolate that he had received from God. No wonder that hard upon this revelation there followed the 'temptation' or testing in the wilderness, when he decided the lines upon which his mission was to be conducted.

*　　*　　*

To these two unveilings it was easy and natural to add a third: that entailed in the first miracle at Cana. This incident of the Epiphany story is no manifestation of humility, nor does it disclose the nature of Christ's mission, but it reveals his power.

It is surely of significance that the evangelist places in such close juxtaposition our Lord's refusal of his Mother's request and his apparently contradictory order to fill the water-pots. The implied suggestion is that he was so closely in touch with his Father that he knew the precise moment at which his hour had come. It is this unique readiness of response to the promptings of the divine will that enabled the Eternal Word to express through him the nature and purpose of God.

So it was that this last manifestation could inaugurate an era in which God's power would be shown through our human nature. Miracles were wrought through Christ's manhood, but they did not close when his visible presence was withdrawn from the earth. Through his body, the Church, they are still performed every time a sacrament is celebrated. The humble physical means are made the vehicle of divine power, and the true mission of Christ for the salvation of man is revealed. Every sacrament is an Epiphany, a true unveiling of Christ, in which his power is perceived by the faithful believer.

THE BOYHOOD OF JESUS

THE boyhood of Jesus has had a singular fascination
for writers and story-tellers throughout the Christian
ages. It began almost at the outset of our era when the
composers of apocryphal gospels invented stories (not all
of them very edifying) about the miracles he was supposed
to have performed as a child. People always want to be
wise above what is written.

Actually all we need to know is packed into that one
sentence of Sunday's gospel: 'Jesus increased in wisdom
and stature and in favour with God and man.' In it is
contained the germ, not only of a biography, but of a
whole doctrine of the Incarnation. The emphasis is upon
the naturalness of his development. One cannot help
noticing the proverbial character of the phraseology. We
talk of a boy growing 'bigger and better': the New Testament talks of 'increasing in wisdom and stature'. Signifi-
cantly there is no reference to moral improvement. We
are merely told that Jesus developed psychologically just
as he did physically.

We are left with the impression of a growth that was
perfect in all its stages—a growth, because the eternal
Word had taken upon himself the form of a man and that
man must grow naturally like other men, and also perfect
because he exhibited the character of perfection proper
to each stage of his growth, as a flower may be perfect
from bud to bloom.

*   *   *

It is striking and instructive that the one incident the
gospels give us from our Lord's boyhood seems to suggest

at first sight that he was not always perfect even with an immature boy's perfection, but could show himself actively disobedient or at least neglectful of his parents' wishes. How could a boy be so thoughtless as to stay away so long from his parents' company?

We must remember the difference between his times and ours. At twelve, a Jewish boy of the period was regarded as much more mature than he would be among ourselves. He was already entering upon manhood. The fact that his parents did not even make sure that he was in the departing caravan, or begin to get anxious about him till the next day, shows that there was a good deal more social freedom than there would be among ourselves. And in any case the notification of time 'after three days', should probably be rendered 'on the third day'.

To stop to listen to the arguments of the rabbis showed intelligence but not precocity. It was a normal element in education, as natural as to listen to a 'brains trust' today. There is no suggestion that Jesus was instructing the rabbis. On the contrary, he was learning from them; and they were surprised and pleased at the intelligence he showed.

*   *   *

That the incident formed no breach with his family we know from the statement that Jesus went home with his parents 'and was subject unto them'. The mother's reproaches could have been expected from any mother. It is the Son's reply that stands out as unique: 'Wist ye not that I must be about my Father's business' or 'in my Father's house?'

The surprise is genuine and revealing. It shows that Jesus had taken seriously and literally what he had been told. Every Jewish boy was taught that God was his

Father: here was one who took his teachers at their word.

We are reminded of a small boy who was not too well over the week-end. 'A good job it was not on Monday', said his mother, 'or you would have missed school.' 'But it is much worse on Sunday', said the boy quite simply, 'because now I must miss church.'

What do we really consider to be the most important things in life? Do we adjust our conduct to the abiding realities, or do we waste our efforts on mere superficialities? Perhaps we need the simple, clear, direct insight of a boy to show us what is real and to set us acting accordingly.

MARRIAGE AT CANA

'WHICH holy estate Christ adorned and beautified with his presence, and first miracle that he wrought, in Cana of Galilee.' The familiar words of the introduction to the marriage service remind us of the way in which the Son of God in his sojourn on earth manifestly gave his approval and blessing to the natural order.

Marriage implies the family, and the family is the unit upon which human society is built. There have been many proposals, and even attempts, by reformers of one kind and another to replace the family with some new structure of society; but they have all failed.

The fact is that the family does indeed form the natural setting for the individual life. It gives security and protection to the child; it gives the adolescent a sense of belonging; it develops the character of the adult. More than any other institution it helps to turn the water of innate capacity into the wine of complete achievement.

And this it does basically because in the family all stand for each. Whatever may be its internal conflicts, the individual member knows that in the last resort the whole family will be behind him in his endeavour to make the best of himself.

*   *   *

St. Paul, recalling that in marriage husband and wife become one flesh, said this was a great mystery; but he was speaking in respect of Christ and his Church. Apparently he meant that, as there is in the Church a mystical or essential union between Christ and his members (for we were 'grafted' into him at baptism), so there is an intermingling of personality between husband and wife in marriage.

If that is so, we see an adequate basis for that mutual care and protection of which we have been speaking. The unity of husband and wife is the basis of the unity of the family. It is the foundation upon which the family is built. And, if that is so in the case of any marriage, how much more must it be so in the wedding of two who are already joined together by their common membership of Christ. St. Paul was bold enough to think of this unity of the Church, the family of God, as something which has existed from all eternity.

There has always been an ideal society in Christ, though men have not seen it actualized. We are fortunate in that it has been brought to our notice through the Incarnation and that we have been introduced into it by Christ. At their best the visible Church and the family are reflections of this ideal state which has always existed 'in the heavens'.

*   *   *

It is not often that the secular State is included in this kind of partnership. But it should be. It is not necessarily the arena of warring factions, nor the seat of tyranny and bureaucracy, nor the scene of violence and of the 'inhumanity of man to man'. It should be an enlargement of the family into which the individual is introduced by no will of his own, but wherein he finds himself wanted and helped.

The advent of the Welfare State has made it possible for people to recognize that even the secular order has its part to play in this essentially Christian task. No doubt many will claim that the State has taken over where the Church has failed. It would be truer to say that the State has followed where the Church has led. Even now it is not clear that the State will be able to make its own services effective without relying upon that spirit of mutual helpfulness which is characteristic of the life of the family and the Church. In this respect the Church is still the leaven intended to leaven the whole lump of society.

Thus nurtured in family, Church and State, we as individuals may be helped to realize our own potentiality, to achieve the end for which God designed us, and so in our turn make our own contribution to the well-being of the whole. All this and much more is implied in the wedding-present Jesus gave the couple so long ago at Cana of Galilee.

UNITY IN THE CHURCH

ST. MATTHEW was intensely interested in the nature of the Church, in the benefits it conferred and the demands it made. It is that interest that connects together the two otherwise unrelated incidents recorded in Sunday's gospel.

The healing of the leper emphasizes the care of Christ and his Church for the untouchable. No one is beyond the reach of Jesus' love. Where other people can think of nothing better to do with an infected man than to keep him from all contact with his fellows, Jesus meets him, heals him and re-introduces him to his place in society.

But this re-entry is not to be effected in any casual manner. The proprieties have to be observed and the regulations satisfied. The examination of the patient and the declaration that he was no longer infectious was the concern of the Church—the Jewish Church, no doubt, but still the Church, the divinely ordained authority in the contemporary world.

St. Matthew's first readers lived at a time when the Christian Church had begun to make clear its own divine authority, and it was becoming, not without some violence, separate from the Church of Judaism. Matthew would wish to tone down the sharpness of the division. He sees one principle of unity and authority running through all God's dispensation, and he therefore emphasizes in this incident the fact that Jesus would allow no discourtesy to be shown to the old-established traditions and customs.

*   *   *

31

If in the case of the leper the evangelist shows the Saviour dealing with an untouchable of Jewish race, in the case of the centurion he shows how a Gentile is brought within the same gracious sphere of love and helpfulness. The officer's care for his servant must have commended him at once to the Master. Jesus shows no hesitation, as one might have expected on the part of a Jew invited to a Gentile house, but says, immediately on hearing of the servant's plight, 'I will come and heal him.'

There is no racial or national discrimination on the part of Jesus, no colour-bar or social exclusiveness. And this, St. Matthew implies, must be the rule for the Church. After all, the work of the Church is to prepare for the coming of the Kingdom; and in the Kingdom of Heaven many will be found from all quarters of the earth, while Jews, the natural inheritors of the Kingdom, will be left in outer darkness.

This unity of all sorts and conditions in Christ is easy enough to accept and applaud while it is concerned with some ideal condition of the future. It is not quite so easy if it meets us in our present circumstances. When we are kneeling at the altar-rail beside someone whose colour, whose habits, whose views, seem utterly alien, if not actually repulsive, do we find it easy to remember our essential oneness in the Church and in Christ Jesus?

*   *   *

We should be helped to overcome our unChristian repugnances if we, like the centurion, could penetrate to the secret of Christ's character. 'I too', he said, 'am a man under authority'—not *in* authority, but *under* authority—'and because I obey my superior officers I can expect other people to obey me.'

Jesus expressed amazement that, where his own people

had failed, a Gentile should have so quickly recognized the spring of his power. It was from his filial consciousness, the sense of being under the immediate direction of his Father, that his strength and decision came.

The world sadly needs in these days of disunity and confusion the witness to this principle of the Christian Church. By drawing close together themselves the churches can help the world to unite. But the churches cannot do that until we, as individuals, are prepared to accept the claims of unity and authority as a genuine standard for our own life and conduct.

CHAOS IN TWO WORLDS

SUNDAY'S gospel, with its two miracles, is intended to illustrate Christ's power in two different spheres, that of physical and that of spiritual force.

In the first incident Jesus is shown fast asleep in the ship when a sudden storm arose. He was so tired out, exhausted, that he did not stir even when the ship was in danger of sinking, and his disciples had to wake him. He seemed surprised at their perturbation, quietly rebuked the wind and the sea, and the storm was allayed.

It would be quite easy to rationalize this story and to say that it was just a remarkable coincidence that the wind dropped at the very moment when Jesus uttered his word. But that is not what we are intended to do. The evangelist expects us to see the incident through the eyes of the disciples, and to be startled into asking what manner of man this was that even the winds and the sea obeyed him.

Even if it were what we call a coincidence we should be expected to recognize the ultimately spiritual constitution of the universe. Behind all the so-called laws of nature there lies in the last resort the will of God. He who was the embodiment of that will was so closely in touch with the forces of nature that even the wind and the waves obeyed him.

*   *   *

The second incident shows the power of Jesus over the world of evil spirits. As we know, this was the great battle-ground over which Jesus had to fight from his baptism to the agony in Gethsemane. The demons were the agents of evil power and they held sway over the minds of men. Anyone who has seen evidence of this belief in the mission field will recognize the vivid reality of the emotions aroused in this story. To show that the evil spirits were themselves subdued by the authority of a good and kind protector of mankind was in itself an act of salvation. It liberated men from the terror of the unseen.

In this case Jesus subdues the demons by a ruse. At their own request he lets them enter the herd of swine; and that results in their immediate destruction. For we may take it that the devils were destroyed as well as the swine.

We may think that there is little meaning for us today in the grim, Oriental humour of this story—Jesus using the devils' own suggestion to destroy them. What has that to say to us? But what about the various types of demon that seem to multiply among us every day—all the forms of robbery and gambling that arise out of the urge to get rich without any honest effort of our own? How many thus afflicted are allowed to follow what seems to be the easy way and so rush upon their own destruction? Here at least, in the longing for sudden and easy wealth, is one form of madness that is not far removed from that of the Gadarene demoniacs.

*   *   *

There is another lesson that we can draw from both these miracles, and that is that God is the God of Peace, and that Jesus is his agent in bringing peace to the world. He calms the tumult, whether it is in the elements of nature or in the hearts of men.

We are sometimes perturbed by the manifestations of violence in nature and we are frightened when we read of the devastation caused by flood and earthquake, or when we have to face their consequences ourselves. But we have to remember that even such violence and terror are ultimately under the will of God. Even though the gaps in our knowledge of evolution are being filled up, God has not been elbowed out of his universe. Without him the world could have no existence at all. It is still in him that we live and move and have our being. Under us are still the everlasting arms. We still find peace and strength in the feel of them, even though the earth be drowned in the depths of the sea.

Similarly, in all the storms that shake our minds, whether of anger, hatred or impatience, we can still find peace if we will remember his presence with us.

HOW TO DEAL WITH THE WEEDS

THE parable of the tares is intended to teach us how to live with our neighbours. It is a simple enough story. A man sows his well-tilled field with perfectly sound wheat, and is surprised to find when the seed grows that it is more than half weed—zizania, darnel or cheat, a kind of plant that looks at first sight very like wheat as it grows. It was far too thick to be accounted for by any natural means. A neighbour who had a grudge against him must have sown it deliberately.

What are they to do, the farm-hands ask; try to get rid of the weeds? A silly question, says a modern critic. But, as any farmer or gardener knows, it was a quite natural question, particularly in days when such weeding was done by hand. But no, the farmer says, if you begin pulling it when it is as thick as that, you are bound to pull up a lot of the wheat with it. Let it grow, and then, when the time for reaping comes, you can cut them down together, separate the darnel and make it up into bundles so that we can at least use it for fuel.

*   *   *

The story as originally told was meant to illustrate the nature of the Kingdom of God. It is like the good field, a sphere in which the will of God is recognized and fully obeyed. But, as the Kingdom exists in this world, it is not always possible to distinguish its members from others who wear the semblance of piety but really live only to serve their own ends.

Matthew's Gospel is the only one that records this precise parable. If we ask why, the answer must be that he was specially interested in the nature of the Church, and in his time it had already been discovered that church membership did not always mean a truly Christian life.

It was thought by the first Christians that, since baptism had cleansed the soul from the faults of the past life, there could be no further falling into serious sin. It was soon found, however, that even baptized people could sometimes be guilty of such sins as apostasy, idolatry or adultery. What must be done with them? Surely they must be excommunicated straight away. That was indeed the method pursued for some time; but it began to be realized that this would mean cutting off souls for whom Christ died.

The early rigorism was gradually relaxed. Means were found of putting wrongdoers to some kind of discipline. Everything was done to make repentance and ultimate restoration possible.

*   *   *

But this is still by no means an out-of-date question. Recent television and newspaper stories have made us aware of sects that demand the clearest possible segregation of their members from all contamination by those who differ from them.

Apart from such extremes it is still a burning question for many a parent. We warn our children against bad companions when they go to school, but we cannot keep them from all undesirable contacts. Later, when the adolescent first goes out into the world, he has to face the same question for himself. He cannot isolate himself from his fellows. To what extent should he associate with those of doubtful character? And, later still, the businessman mixes with all kinds of people: how is he to keep himself unspotted from the world?

The answer of the parable is that we must take the

world as we find it. We are taught to pray that we may not be led into temptation but delivered from evil. Yet Jesus himself refused to ask that his followers should be taken out of the world. Only by contact with our fellows can our character be strengthened and our mission to the world be accomplished.

We must preserve an inner citadel, a life of hidden communication with God. We know that there will be a judgment, that God's field must one day be cleansed of noxious weeds. In the meantime we must use all our contacts to win our acquaintances to God's side. So shall we, with them, be garnered as wheat at the last.

THE END OF THE WORLD

Epiphany VI   *St. Matthew* 24. 23

THE thought of the end of the world has had an irresistible attraction for all generations.

The Jews especially, with their long-standing interest in prophecy, were prone to look into the ultimate future whenever present circumstances proved too much for them. As we can see from the book of Daniel and from Revelation, as well as from books outside the canon, the vivid pictures they drew in this state of mind developed into a highly specialized literature with its own characteristic language and figures of speech.

We must always remember this quality of 'apocalyptic' when we are reading passages from the gospels relating to the end. Jesus is talking in this special kind of language, which is highly pictorial and poetical.

Thus in the gospel for Epiphany VI, which we read on Sunday, he begins by warning his hearers against false alarms. They must not think that Christ has come in the wilderness or in some secret enclosed place, as John the Baptist or the members of the Qumran community may have thought. When he comes it will be suddenly, but with as much certainty as, when a beast falls dead, a vulture appears in the sky. It will also be accompanied by startling phenomena in the natural world. The sun will disappear from the heavens and consequently the moon will give no light. And all the stars will be shaken in their fixed places and the planets will deviate from their proper courses.

*   *   *

It is doubtful whether any of this was ever intended

to be taken literally. Actually it is not fundamentally different from the picture a modern scientist might draw if he were trying to depict the end of the world through the clashing of planets. But the picture, as drawn, was already stereotyped in the literature of the day. It is not difficult to see the lesson it was intended to convey.

First, the coming of the end could not be precisely timed, and one must not be misled by fanatics into thinking it was already here. But, though it could not be exactly foretold, the coming was absolutely certain, and no one should forget it.

Further, when it does come, everyone will know of it. It will not be some esoteric experience, known only to a chosen few; it will be obvious and universal. As the lightning, with its sudden, vivid flash, illuminates the whole sky from pole to pole, even on the darkest night, so everyone will be suddenly aware when the Son of Man has come.

What will be the 'sign' of the Son of Man we are not told, but at least it will be the signal that the long concession to evil is over and that goodness has at last taken command over all the earth. The Son of Man comes with power and great glory.

*   *   *

What is specially intriguing to a modern about this way of emphasizing the certainty and suddenness of the end is that it is so completely different from our normal unconcern. Whatever we might say about such a conception if we were driven to offer an opinion, the fact is that we habitually act as if there were no such threat at all.

True, we may realize that as individuals we face the fate that is here pictured for the whole world. Death may be as sudden and unexpected as the end of the material universe is here said to be. In fact there have been commentators who would take the whole picture out of its cosmic context and relate it solely to the life of the private person.

There is, however, another way of looking at this picture. The Fourth Gospel, for instance, does not think of the final issue as coming, so to speak, at the end of a line. For St. John the 'beyond' is about us all the time. We are as near to eternity at any one moment as at any other.

We live indeed in two worlds, the temporal and the eternal. Even while we are busy about the affairs of the former we must not forget the latter. In that way we shall be less perturbed about the end. When the material barriers are at last thrown down, we shall find ourselves in a sphere with which we have long been familiar.

THE VINEYARD

'THE kingdom of Heaven is like.' It was the conventional beginning to Jesus' stories, very much like our own contemporary opening. 'Once upon a time.' As soon as the crowd heard it, they would gather closer to hear what the Teacher had to say.

In the present case the opening sentence sounded improbable enough. 'The Kingdom of Heaven is like a man. . . .' How can a Kingdom be like a man? However, it is a man in action, a wealthy vine-grower trying to find sufficient labour for the harvesting of his grapes. The story goes on to describe the conditions of employment in the vineyard. It is the vineyard rather than the man that is the replica of the Kingdom.

To the hearers the comparison must have seemed revolutionary. It completely reverses the common picture of the Messianic Kingdom. Here is no life of ease and plenty after the destruction of every enemy, as is described, for instance, in the Dead Sea Scrolls, but one of arduous toil.

Thus it has at least this to recommend it, that it is a condition of full employment. No one remains without work; no one is without pay; no one goes hungry.

But even in the method of payment there is something odd. The labourers are not paid according to the number of hours they have worked. There is one fixed payment for all alike at whatever time they are taken on. It is certainly an upheaval in the normal sense of justice.

*   *   *

If we ask what the hearers were expected to make of

43

all this, we must bear in mind two different audiences. There were first the bystanders to whom Jesus spoke, and then later there were the congregations for whom Matthew chose out this story and inserted it in his gospel.

If Jesus' intention was to remind his hearers that the ideal state of existence is not one of leisured ease but of steady, consistent work, Matthew might have wished his hearers to remember that there was work for every Christian still. Two generations had gone by; Jesus had not yet returned; the world was not yet won.

There was therefore work for all still in the Master's vineyard. Good Christian people must not rest idle while there was so much to be done. The duty of preparing the way for the coming of the Kingdom was the task of all. The whole Christian community without exception must unite in the effort to complete it.

Possibly there is also a side-reference to jealousies in the congregation. The grumbling of the earliest labourers because they got no greater reward than the late-comers may have reminded the Jewish members in Matthew's congregation a little uncomfortably of the things they had said about Gentiles who had been admitted to the Church on easy terms. Ought these late converts really to enjoy all the privileges of the original Jewish members?

*   *   *

This thought brings the teaching of the parable out of the communal into the individual sphere. The story is repeated not merely for the congregation as a whole but for each individual. What has it to say to me?

First, surely, that in my own Christian life I must be a worker. I must recognize my responsibility, take it seriously, and not remain idle while the rest do the work.

And then I must not expect a nicely calculated payment for my services. There is one reward for all alike in the commendation of the Master and the privilege of being in his presence. There is no room for repining or envy if others seem to have an easier lot than ourselves.

And finally, I must be prepared to give my 'utmost for the highest'. It may be late in the day and physically I may not be the man I was, but God wants me as I am and the whole of me.

These are not bad thoughts to have in our minds as we enter upon our preparation for the season of Lent.

SOWER, SEED AND SOIL

EVERYONE loves a good story, and nowhere has the
art of story-telling been brought to a finer pitch of
excellence than in the East. Jesus, who lived so close to
the heart of his people, understood their tastes very well
and used his knowledge in the proclamation of his good
news.

A parable, we used to be taught at school, is an earthly
story with a heavenly meaning. Some of the greatest
scholars today are coming round to the conclusion that
that is perhaps as good a definition as any. All the great
story-tellers, like the great dramatists, intend their narrative to be understood at more than one level. T. S. Eliot
is a typical modern example of a playwright who tells a
story of considerable interest on the surface but also
presenting an underlying world of profound truths.

The parables of Jesus function on two levels, the everyday
incident and the spiritual experience. But how are the
two linked? Here there is a difference of opinion. Some
scholars think that the key to the interpretation is simplicity: in each story Jesus has one point, and one only,
that he wishes to drive home. Others think that a better
key is the allegorical interpretation, in accordance with
which every detail is capable of conveying its own part
of the message.

*   *   *

The interesting thing is that, in the parable of the
Sower as given in the Gospels, we are encouraged to use
both methods. We are first told the story and given the
opportunity to make our own simple deduction from it,

and then taken aside and in a sort of appendix given an allegorical explanation in detail.

Taking the simpler method first, we are tempted to think of the story as merely illustrative of Jesus' own life and teaching. He himself was the Sower, delivering his message to all and sundry and meeting with very divers kinds of reception. It would, however, be hardly like Jesus' usual method, merely to recount some piece of autobiography without leaving his hearers some lesson to draw for themselves.

If, then, there is some one simple lesson to be drawn, is it not that anyone who seeks to proclaim God's message must expect to meet with a very mixed reception? It is not going to be all plain sailing, just because we are on an errand from God. We shall have our successes and failures. We must not be either optimistic or pessimistic but just realistic, knowing that in the end it is God who will give the harvest in his own good time.

That, at any rate, would be a lesson the evangelists would be anxious to put before their readers of the second Christian generation. They were now responsible for the spread of the gospel. They must not think it was going to be an easy task. But they must persevere. They must never miss an opportunity. They must sow beside all waters. God himself would give the increase.

*   *   *

Then comes the allegorical explanation in the appendix, with its suggestion that those specially close to Christ may see further into the meaning of his discourse than others.

In this detailed explanation the emphasis is subtly changed. The seed is the Word of God, but the emphasis is entirely on the character of the soil. We are given a psychological analysis of four different types of hearers whom any preacher or evangelist may meet.

The first, represented by the hard path, consists of the people who casually hear the message but give no heed to it at all; it never has the chance of sinking in. The second are the shallow, easily enthusiastic people, who are all agog at the first hearing of some new thing but whose keenness rapidly evaporates.

The third are the troubled people, those who are full of worries and anxieties, or the pleasure-seekers, who are so busy chasing after a good time that they miss all that makes life most worth living. The fourth are the sincere people, those of 'an honest and good heart'. They are the ones who will nourish the Word and give it the opportunity of producing fruit to life eternal.

GATE TO THE KINGDOM

ON the threshold of Lent, we are given in the gospel
for Quinquagesima a quick, summary view of the
shadowed path by which Jesus entered into his glory. We
look straight out of the darkness of his Passion through
the gloomy misunderstanding of his disciples into the
light of the power of his Kingdom, as depicted in the
healing of the blind man.

First there is the announcement of the necessity for his
humiliating death. That is how things must be done in
order to fulfil God's plan of salvation. Long ago the
prophets had interpreted the history of their people in
such a way as to show how God was using them to bring
a blessing to all the nations of the earth. One at least of
them had seen that this benefit could be conferred, not
by establishing a world-wide empire to which the nations
should all be made subject, but only by so intense a
sympathy and co-operation as would involve bearing the
utmost calamity on their behalf. The songs of the Suffering
Servant, embodying this ideal of vicarious endurance,
had been the most neglected portion of the Second Isaiah,
although isolated communities such as that of Qumran,
as we learn from the Dead Sea Scrolls, may have meditated upon the idea and its implications.

But here is Jesus applying the character of the Suffering
Servant to himself and teaching that, if he is to fulfil
his Father's will and carry out the plan to make his people
a blessing to the world, he must inevitably suffer and die.

*   *   *

And here are his disciples, standing with him in the

shadow of his impending calamity, but not understanding in the least what it all means. This is the most difficult of all situations for both teacher and pupils, for both leader and led, when a truth so glaring to the one cannot be shared by the others. If those others are called upon to face great odds without properly knowing the reason why, and yet maintain, even blindly, their trust in their leader, this is a severe trial to both patience and faith. And the problem can only be resolved in the light of practical experience.

That is, no doubt, one of the purposes for which we are expected to face the austerity of Lent. We are still in the shadow of only partial understanding. We see in a glass darkly. To clear our vision we need to escape from the distortion produced by merely material interests and self-indulgent pleasures. We must enter into a position where some hardship is voluntarily accepted, not just for the sake of improving our own temper or character or chance of heaven, but precisely in order to enter into the spirit of our Lord's own self-sacrifice by deliberately forgoing our own convenience for the sake of others. This may help us a little through actual experience to enter into the mind of the Master.

* * *

But God tempers the wind to the shorn lamb. Even in seeming desolation he does not leave his own without some evidence of himself. The declaration of the necessity of suffering and death has hardly been made, the mis-understanding of the disciples has hardly become visible, when the characteristic glory of the Kingdom is revealed in the healing of the blind man. Here was one who was in utter darkness, who could see nothing at all, and upon whom in answer to such faith as he had, the full light of day was made to burst. So at the end of the dark road of suffering waited the light of Paradise for the Son of Man.

So, too, for us waits the glory of Easter beyond the gloom of Lent. It is a parable of our life on this earth. But we who belong to the number of the redeemed know already that the glory of the Kingdom is our true abiding-place. Our citizenship is in heaven. Even here in the shadow we are pilgrims following our Leader towards the light, which already casts its glow on our faces and makes supportable the hardness and unevenness of our path.

THE TEMPTATIONS

IT is appropriate that, as we stand on the threshold of
Lent, we should be set to consider our Lord's temptations. As we ourselves enter upon an intensive struggle
with the enemies of the soul, nothing could be more
inspiring than to consider how Jesus himself met and
defeated those self-same forces at the outset of his ministry.

His first temptation was to put his own personal needs
in the forefront. After all, we might say, a man can do
no proper work unless he is decently fit himself. How can
he put energy into any task if he is starving with hunger?
This temptation Jesus resists with the reflection that man's
real food is not the bread he eats but the voice that comes
to him from God. It is that which supports and sustains
him in his work and in his aspirations. It is only as he
listens to that voice that he can be in a position to do
anything of real significance. God's word is the staff and
power of life.

Our endeavour, then, through Lent will be to listen
more carefully for that voice. We may even have to think
a little less about our material needs, our hopes and
ambitions for ourselves, in order to provide opportunity
to let God speak to us in the inner recesses of our soul.

*   *   *

If the first temptation was to self-pity, the second was to
spiritual pride or presumption. Had not Jesus the promise
of God's protection? Then why not draw upon it in order
to make some great public demonstration and to ensure
that his task of winning the assent of the people would be
so much easier? Why not throw himself in the sight of

the crowd from the parapet of the temple, confident that
God would see that he alighted without harm?

To this Jesus can only reply: 'Thou shalt not tempt
the Lord thy God.' No man has any right to put God to
the test. Nor has any man the right to think that he stands
in so privileged a position with God that he can afford to
neglect the ordinary laws and customs of everyday life.

We, like everyone else, must learn to understand how
the world works and to accept its ordered machinery.
We cannot dictate terms to God. We dare not ask: 'Why
have you treated me thus?' We must live our lives and
bear our burdens according to the universal rules,
knowing that the power of God will be displayed not in
lifting us out of them, but in enabling us to live courage-
ously and profitably in the world as it is.

*   *   *

The third and final temptation was almost the exact
opposite of the second. Instead of suggesting an act of
presumption it suggests an unworthy compromise. Part
of the subtlety of the tempation lies in the fact that not
all compromise is bad. Without compromise no two people
could ever live together and scarcely any business could
ever be done.

But in this case the suggested compromise was evil.
It was to recognize the supremacy of the devil in what he
considered his own sphere. It could so easily be done.
Business is business and politics is politics; all's fair in
love and war. So we say, and in saying it we have already
suggested that there are many spheres in which the strict
application of Christian principles does not seem to work.

Certainly there are many instances in which we find
it hard to tell whether, in adopting a certain line, we are
acknowledging the rule of what is essentially evil. Here
the only way out is to lay the issue before God: 'Him

E

only shalt thou serve.' We have useful guides in the Bible and the Church. We may be sure that, if we do only what we seriously believe we have learned from God, we are not likely to offend against him or our own souls.

Thus are our Lord's temptations translated into our own terms. Our meditation upon them this Lent ought to bring us at least a little closer to him in sympathy and understanding.

HUMILIATIONS

Lent II   *St. Matthew* 15. 21

JESUS' contacts with members of non-Jewish races
seem to have been comparatively rare. They excite
all the greater interest for that reason.

St. Mark and St. Matthew are specially interested in
the case of the Greek-speaking Syrophœnician woman—
St. Mark because he wishes to make clear the attitude of
the Messiah to non-Jews, and St. Matthew because he
wishes to show how the old prophecies are fulfilled in Jesus.
That may explain why the former gives the current name
of the woman's national standing (Syrophœnician) while
the latter reverts to the old-fashioned title and calls her
a 'woman of Canaan'.

To us, with our instinctively universalist notions, it
may seem odd that any point should be raised about our
Lord's attitude to foreigners. We are indeed inclined to
be a little shocked by his apparent aloofness in this
instance. How does it square with the invitation, 'Come
unto me *all* ye that labour and are heavy laden'?

The fact is that Jesus' primary mission on earth was
to the Jews. They were the people long before chosen by
God to be the instruments of his special revelation. That
principle still holds good when the Son of God, as the
culmination of that revelation, becomes incarnate.

*   *   *

We can well imagine that this particularism would
arouse some questioning among the people for whom the
Evangelists wrote. Indeed, we know from what St. Paul
tells us that there had been a considerable controversy
over this very question. How far and on what terms were

the privileges of the gospel to be thrown open to non-Jews?

When Matthew's gospel was read out in the presence of the worshipping congregation, there would be Jews and Gentiles listening to it side by side. Did the Jews feel or show any superiority to their Gentile neighbours? Did the Gentiles suffer from an inferiority complex as interlopers or gate-crashers? We are told in *Acts* 15 that the apostles had already sent a circular letter to the young churches about this situation. But the uneasy feeling might still remain; and the account of this miracle would show how Jesus himself had dealt with the question.

In the first place, there was no disguising the fundamental fact: Jesus was sent first to the Jew. Second, however, this priority did not preclude acts of mercy to any foreigner in need who was brought in contact with him.

What then was the criterion by which the claim on Jesus could be judged? Faith, and faith only. Trust in Christ, rely on him, recognize your dependence on him, and the floodgates of his kindness and love are open to you. Whatever may be your race, or colour, or place of origin, or situation, or position in society, have faith in him and your utmost need will be satisfied.

*   *   *

That is no doubt the kind of lesson the miracle would convey to the contemporary Church. But it does not exhaust the meaning of the miracle for us. We cannot help noticing the way in which Jesus tested, almost teased, the woman. At first he refuses to answer, then seems to endorse the disciples' movement to send her away, and finally uses the harsh comparison between children and dogs.

Nothing, however, puts the woman off. She has a sick daughter; she means if possible to get her healed; and she will put up with anything to get her errand of mercy fulfilled. So does Jesus draw out and strengthen her gift of perseverance.

But what humiliation the woman has to endure before reaching the goal of final perseverance. There are some graces that we can only learn the hard way. Humility, we are told, comes by humiliations. We must learn this Lent not to be bitter or resentful about them, but to use them as a means of coming closer to Christ.

BATTLE ROYAL

ONE of the main aspects under which the New Testament envisages the messianic mission of Jesus is as a campaign against the world of evil spirits. A generation or two ago, we should have said that this had little meaning for modern man. But the recent discoveries in the realm of psychology, with their revelation of personal depths below the surface of consciousness, and their emphasis on the power of mind over matter, have put us once again *en rapport* with the characteristic thought of the first century.

*   *   *

If the initial engagement in our Lord's campaign was the Temptation, when he defied Satan and laid down his own plan for his mission, St. Luke leaves us in no doubt that the great central battle was as depicted in the gospel for next Sunday. The stage for the decisive argument is carefully set. Jesus had cast out a devil of dumbness. He was immediately challenged on the most subtle of all grounds, not that he had not performed the cure successfully, but that he had only done it by black magic, that is, with the aid of the leader of evil spirits.

His reply is threefold: (a) that there is no division in the Satanic forces, (b) that in making the charge his interlocutors are calling in question the exorcisms performed by their own rabbis, and (c) that the number and effectiveness of his cures are surely good evidence that in him the messianic kingdom has already begun to appear.

*   *   *

Jesus then describes the success of his campaign in a vivid parable. Satan is like a noble guarding his castle and trusting in the amount and modernity of his munitions, but when a stronger neighbour comes along he not only sacks the castle but leaves its owner without any weapons of offence or defence.

Having thus pictured his own victory as complete, Jesus challenges his hearers. On whose side are they? They cannot sit on the fence: there is no neutrality in this war. If they do not declare definitely for him, they have in effect already decided against him. The psychological disposition is the decisive factor. Here then is a question we must keep before ourselves this Lent. Is our decision for him definite and sincere?

*   *   *

Another question for our Lenten pondering is suggested by the following comparison. A person who has been cured of demoniacal possession is in a dubious position. He is like a host who has just said good-bye to an unwelcome guest and has got the room tidy again for some new traveller. He must take care that it is quickly occupied, or the former visitor may return, bringing with him a number of boon-companions to demand hospitality.

That is a lesson for recidivists all the world over. And which of us at some time or other has not belonged to that unhappy class? The remedy lies in what used to be called 'the expulsive power of a new affection'. Self-denial is not enough. The room left vacant by our negative rules must be filled by things that are true and lovely and of good report.

*   *   *

How this may be done is further shown in reply to the fussy and sentimental woman who said what a marvellous thing it must be to the mother of Jesus. That, he said, was not the point. It is not physical relationship that matters, but spiritual. Listen to the divine instruction and try to live up to it: that will fill your minds and days, put you in the closest relationship to God, and leave no room for evil to enter. By such means we shall be wholly committed to the army of Christ.

THE FAMILY TABLE

AT first sight there seems little in common between the feeding of the five thousand and that 'mothering' in family and Church which forms the main subject of our thoughts on this Sunday. But actually there are connections, not too hard to trace, on three different levels.

First on the lowest and most material level, that of the meal itself. It is one of the most necessary functions of every mother to see that her children are properly fed. That most necessary function we see Jesus himself performing in this miracle. Jesus' care for the bodily needs of his hearers is a little unexpected. One does not expect the modern evangelist to bother overmuch about the meals of his hearers! But it is entirely in keeping with what we know of our Lord's character.

He who cares for the sparrows and taught us to pray for our daily bread is not likely to overlook the physical needs of any of his children. In this respect the Church, the mother of us all, has followed his example, with some lapses, through the ages. We must ask ourselves whether we as individuals do the same. Are we this Lent doing what we can to help feed the starving millions?

*   *   *

A second level on which the miracle is appropriate to Mothering Sunday is its illustration of the Jerusalem which is above. The author of the Fourth Gospel does not narrate the miracle merely as an historical episode. He uses it as an illustration of the Kingdom the Messiah has come to introduce.

Spiritually this is the condition of peace, power and plenty in which those who come to Mount Sion will habitually dwell. It is quite different, as the epistle points out, from the condition of those who dwelt at the foot of Sinai, where there were thunder and lightning and the terrors of the Law.

The contrast between Sion and Sinai is not so much geographical as psychological. God's new family, the whole family of Christ's people throughout the world, does not live under law but under grace, not in bondage but in freedom, not in fear but in love.

The burden of much of the teaching we hear today is that the Church is in danger of slipping back into the condition of legalism, of slavery to custom and prejudice. We may not agree with much that is said, but at least the warning is salutary. We are the dear children of God, and love, both to him and to the other children, must characterize his whole family and every member of it.

*   *   *

And when can this love be more spontaneously manifested than round the common table? It is clear that St. John, in telling this story, intends it to be seen against the background of the Eucharist. He uses it in his famous sixth chapter to lead into the discussion on the Bread of Life and the Flesh which is meat indeed, our true sustenance for the journey of life, both here and hereafter.

So we are brought back on a new level to the thought of Mothering Sunday. Like St. John himself, we hover between the material and the spiritual. The meals the mother provides out of her loving care are each one a current symbol of the Eucharist, the common meal of the children of God. And that in its turn is the means by which we feed upon God himself, the author and sustainer of all life, physical and spiritual.

Here then is our incentive to make us think more carefully of our Communions this Lent and to make more careful preparation for them. If we do so treat them, they will bring us closer to God and to the constant recollection of his parental care for us all. And that in its turn will lead us to ask how we are reflecting that care in our regard for the other members of the Family among whom we live.

MEANING OF THE PASSION

PASSION SUNDAY holds the crucifix before our eyes.
It impels us to look at the Passion in the round before
we enter into its details. It induces us to consider the
meaning of the Cross. For what purpose did Jesus 'go up
to Jerusalem' and deliver himself to death? There were
no doubt many reasons, but three stand out distinctly.

First, he must give to a hard, brutish and arrogant
world an example of love. It was the purpose of God to
disclose through Jesus his own true nature. How far Jesus
was conscious of this over-ruling purpose we need not
enquire. But we do know that he was aware that he must
'fulfil all righteousness', and that in his own human life
there were forces at work that did not admit of any easy,
temporal explanation. By doing as he did he would let
all generations see into the heart of God.

At the same time he would manifest his own love both
to his Father and to the world. He was ready to give himself to the uttermost, even if it meant yielding himself to
men's will. He lost his own life in the attempt to save
theirs. What greater evidence could there be of love?

*   *   *

Second, by his death Jesus opened the way for reconciliation between God and man. He broke down the
aloofness of humankind, their unwillingness to admit their
mistakes and their sin. As we look at the Cross and see in it
the effect of our waywardness, it is no longer difficult to
say we are sorry. We would wish only to atone for our
faults.

The means of that atonement Jesus himself provides.

What God could not do while we remained cold, hard and aloof, he can do at once when we are induced by the love shown upon the Cross to open our hearts to him. In this way, Jesus not only expiates our sins but propitiates the Father. God's love has not changed; it has been there all the time; but, whereas we had barricaded ourselves against it, it has now full and free access to our hearts.

This is what is meant by the 'sacrifice' of Christ. Everyone wishes to express love, affection, esteem by some gift. All through history men had shown their worship of God in the offering of sacrifice. Here Jesus gathers up the age-long offerings of his people and the desires of all who were still to come, and holds them up to his Father in the comprehensive sacrifice of the Cross. In that offering all the heroism of all that have ever given their lives for others is contained and consecrated.

*   *   *

Third, by his Cross Jesus effected a union between God and man. Upon this the whole process of salvation depended. The work of our redemption is not something that happened two thousand years ago. We cannot be saved by what happens outside us in either space or time. The whole drama of the Passion must be enacted within the circle of our own personality. We are reconciled to God through Jesus Christ not merely in Jerusalem in A.D. 29, but here and now.

This situation Jesus showed in unforgettable symbol on the night before his Crucifixion. He had looked forward with great longing to this meal with his disciples. In the course of it he broke the bread and said 'This is my body', and passed round the cup saying 'This is my blood', telling them to eat and drink.

Could there be any more realistic way of affirming their essential unity with himself? As food and drink become part of our physical frame, so Jesus becomes part of our personality. Being one with him, we suffer and die with him. The evil world with its passions and its weakness is no longer the environment in which we live. Our true life is hid with Christ in God, in whom is life and health and peace.

FOUR REPORTS

Sunday next before Easter   *St. Matthew* 27. 1

THE earliest Christians must have pondered long over
the events of what we now call Holy Week. The
evangelists give us a much fuller account of those last
days than of any other period of the Lord's earthly life.
Palm Sunday acts as a kind of prologue to the drama.
Each of the gospel-writers has his own way of looking
at it.

St. Mark's is the basic account. Brief and clear as his
narrative is, he infuses into it an air of mystery as he tells
how the Messiah came to the capital city of his race to
face martyrdom. The preparations move so smoothly
that it almost seems as if everything was arranged by a
divine ordinance. Jesus is greeted as the restorer of his
people about to renew the glories of the Kingdom of
David. But all he does is to go up to the Temple, look
around, and then retire to Bethany for the night with the
Twelve.

*   *   *

St. Luke's is the next account, and he deliberately
amplifies the narrative of Mark. He tells of Jesus weeping
at sight of the city, of his prophecy that it would soon
be destroyed, of the Pharisees' remonstrance over the
cheering of the crowds, and of his magnificent wrath at
the abuse of the Temple.

To this Evangelist Jesus is not so much the martyred
Messiah as the great heroic teacher who has a message for
all, rich and poor alike, and who is of the utmost significance to Gentile as well as to Jew, to the proud Roman as
well as to the Galilean peasant.

Jesus' tears over the city and his prophecy of doom should make an especial appeal to us in these days when the world is in so great a turmoil, when the efforts of statesmen seem destined to endless frustration and mankind seems bent on its own destruction. We must try to bear with Christ some of the sorrow of the world, and in so bearing it help to provide a way of escape.

*   *   *

St. Matthew has a rather different way of thinking about Jesus. He is a writer who has meditated much on the ancient scriptures of his people. He believed that Jesus had come to fulfil the purpose of God in training the Jews to be his instrument for the salvation of the world. He sees not only in the main events of Jesus' life but even in its details the fulfilment of prophecies made long before.

Consequently he is not content merely to repeat the events of the day; he also shows how they fit in with the ancient writings. So in telling how humbly Jesus rode into Jerusalem he cannot help pointing out how exactly it suits the old prophecy of Zechariah. As St. Luke had also done, he remembers how the traders in the Temple were repeating what had happened in the time of Isaiah: they were turning the house of prayer into a 'robbers' cave'. And later he sees in the chants of the choir-boys, recalling the hosannas of the crowd, a fulfilment of the Psalmist's words, 'Out of the mouths of babes and sucklings thou hast perfected praise.'

Here, more than in the other gospels, we get the sense of excitement in the city. It was not just on the road leading into Jerusalem but in the town itself that people were stirred up by an expectancy that great things were to happen and the purpose of God was to be fulfilled. Perhaps we in our own day catch something of this feeling of destiny, and even when we are most disturbed about the state of the world remember that God is working his purpose out. We are the instruments of God, and he can never fail.

*   *   *

Finally, St. John carries the thought back beyond the Old Testament into eternity. To him always Jesus is the incarnation of the eternal Word of God. Even the Crucifixion itself is part of his glorification. So particularly in this prologue of Palm Sunday he notices how the Pharisees are complaining that 'the whole world has gone after him'. And to the Greeks who ask to see him, Jesus explains: 'The hour has come for the Son of Man to be glorified.'

F

CHRIST OUR PASSOVER

TODAY we arrive at the Pasch, the combined commemoration of the Crucifixion and the Resurrection.
In modern times we are accustomed to distinguish sharply
between the two events and to deride the journalists when
they appear to confuse them. But anciently they were
coupled together and regarded as the contrasted aspects
of one great saving event.

The combination goes back as far as the Old Testament,
for the Pasch is simply the Passover itself combined with
the Feast of Unleavened Bread, both together commemor-
ating the delivery from Egypt. In early Christian times
the combination received some justification from the
gospel of St. John, which recorded the saying: 'I, if I be
lifted up, will draw all men unto me.' This great and
memorable saying included a reference to both the
Crucifixion and the subsequent triumph of Jesus.

The double event marked the decisive turning-point
in the history of revelation, and indeed of the world.
We are accustomed to think of our lives as fundamentally
affected by it; but we do not always remember that the
whole of the New Testament was written in the light of it.
Indeed, it is obviously difficult for the evangelists not
to have it in their thoughts as they recount the events
of the Lord's earthly life.

*   *   *

This week at least we are encouraged to hold both
thoughts together, and derive special understanding of
their meaning and inspiration from their sharp contrast.

The utter gloom of Black Friday is not without its

own promise of comfort, or we could never have called it Good Friday. The physical darkness of the moment of the dereliction is lightened for the careful reader by the recollection that the cry 'My God, my God, why hast thou forsaken me?' is a quotation from the twenty-second psalm, and is hardly to be taken literally. The past tense that Jesus uses (Why *didst* thou forsake me?) suggests, too, that the sensation of utter loneliness, of being abandoned to bear his physical and mental anguish alone, was already over.

Certainly the sense of the Father's presence was speedily recovered, and at the end Jesus can repeat the evening prayer he had probably said from boyhood: 'Father, into thy hands I commend my spirit.' We can reflect that because Jesus has trodden this way before us we are assured of his comfort at our latter end. As the darkness engulfs us and the waters close over our head, we shall feel his presence with us and his strong arm supporting us to the other side.

*   *   *

If that is one part of the Paschal lesson, Easter comes with its assurance that there is another part, that the Christian dies but to live. In every generation we need that assurance. It never can be easy to maintain a conviction that seems so little supported by our senses. But Jesus, by his Resurrection, brought life and immortality to light. We must grasp the revealed truth by faith—the same kind of faith by which we rely upon wife or husband or friend. We must hold it so firmly that it becomes a conviction, an attitude of mind that forces us to act.

Thus, like the writers of the New Testament, we shall find our whole life affected by our belief. We shall recognize ourselves as pilgrims returning home, and all our thoughts and habits will be those of our homeland.

Our life is hid with Christ in God. And that life is a risen life displaying the power of the Resurrection in its everyday concerns. The assurance of its presence within us we have in that 'feast upon a sacrifice' which is our Easter Communion. Here is our feast of unleavened bread following upon the self-offering of Good Friday. The Old and New Testament symbols intertwine as we keep the double commemoration. The whole of revelation comes here to a point. Christ our Passover is sacrificed for us; therefore let us keep the feast.

THREEFOLD RESURRECTION

Easter Day   *St. John* 20. 1

THE first meaning of Easter is that it guarantees for
those who are in Christ a joyful immortality beyond
the grave. It is this that gives purpose to our existence on
earth, and makes life worth living. It gives to our individual lives a dignity and importance that they could not
otherwise possess. We are born not only for time but for
eternity.

We know that being in Christ we do not have to wait
for death to usher us into that higher state of life. It is
something that begins here and now. We can already
enjoy the enhanced quality of life, if only we remember
whose and what we are.

What is true of ourselves is true of countless others also.
We do not lose our friends or our relatives when they die.
The ties of blood and friendship that are established here
are not destined to be broken by death. The grave has
been revealed to be not a terminus but a gate. On the
other side of it are the many mansions where we must
meet again those whom we had loved and lost awhile.
If there is no marriage in heaven it is not because ties are
looser there, but because the fusion of individual per-
sonalities there transcends anything of which our coarser,
earthbound existence can have experience.

*   *   *

But the meaning of Easter does not stop with the
individual. It has a world-wide, cosmic effect. It represents an epoch-making event in the course of world
history. It is nothing less than the victory of life over death
here throughout the physical plane of existence. It is

the triumph of the great affirmation of life over against the negation of death.

This is why we must continue to emphasize the importance of the physical resurrection. Christ's body was part of the material universe. Inasmuch as it was raised from the tomb, it became a kind of first-fruits of a world freed from mortality. It guarantees a future use for every created thing, even in a new state of existence.

A great French writer has tried to link this piece of revelation with the scientific theory of evolution. In his view the whole universe in which life, in all its manifold forms, has been evolved, culminating in man, is moving towards an ultimate perfection involving a hitherto unrealized degree of spiritualization. The resurrection change in the body of Christ is an earnest of the transformation of the material universe.

This, we are told, does not take place involuntarily. Now that man is able to take a conscious and deliberate part in his own evolution, society as a whole must give itself to the task. Only if we share in the risen life of Christ here and now can we assist, instead of frustrating, the grand design of the universe.

*   *   *

The third important aspect of Easter is the part it played in the bringing to life of the Christian Church. We know from the gospels how it changed the disciples from a band of frightened refugees hiding in the back streets of Jerusalem into a vitalized company ready to spread the good news throughout Palestine and the world.

Some scholars who are not able to accept as literally true the story of the empty tomb are ready to see in this emergence of the Church the real significance of what they call the Easter event. We may well pity their lack of faith in the historical narrative, but we may be thankful for their positive teaching.

The French writer to whom we have already referred seizes on this point of view to further his own argument. The Church is the new body of Christ risen with Life from the dead, associated at one and the same time with the Christ reigning from Heaven and with the consecrated bread and wine on the altar. The Church, with its combined spiritual and material elements, thus becomes a fresh and continuous impulse in that process of evolution which will end in the fulness of God and the perfection of heaven.

We who rejoice at this time in the triumph of our own individual rising with Christ must not let our thoughts stop there. We must go on to thank him for the universal victory he has won, and ask for grace and power to help make it come true in the daily life of everyone within our reach.

PEACE AND POWER

THE first Peace that Jesus bestowed upon his disciples on the evening of Easter Day arose from the conviction of his Resurrection. He showed them his hands and his side; so there could be no mistake in identification. He who stood before them now was no vague apparition, but the very Jesus with whom they had walked and talked and whom they had seen crucified.

But there was a difference. The wounds no longer bled. They could be touched without causing any anguish. He was the same Jesus, but transformed. He had appeared suddenly before them even though the door was locked. The body of his resurrection was capable of new and strange powers.

The change in perception was symbolic of the whole attitude of the disciples. Henceforth they looked upon everything from the point of view of the Resurrection. We can see it in the gospel narratives of the Lord's mission, especially that of St. John. Although the story is vividly told, there is an atmosphere of triumph and peace that could not have been there throughout. We are expressly told, 'These things they understood not until he was risen from the dead.'

The triumphant peace of Easter has made all things new. And that, we must remember, is the peace in which we still live today.

*   *   *

It no doubt seemed odd that Jesus should utter a second Peace. After all, it was the normal greeting, as it is still in some parts of the East today, Salaam, our Good-evening, the Hebrew Shalom, peace. And one doesn't usually say Good-evening twice to the same people. It was no doubt repeated here with the intention of removing the phrase from the sphere of a commonplace salutation and emphasizing the content of the word Peace.

In effect, it established the right atmosphere for the solemn commission that was now to be conferred. 'As my Father has sent me, even so send I you.' To express such a sentiment was to constitute the Church and announce its marching orders. Those cowering, timorous disciples, huddling together in a locked room for mutual reassurance and protection, were first given peace and assurance, and then made into a formal body, and told to set out on a divine, world-saving mission.

They were to carry on the work of their Master. He deliberately makes them sharers in the work the Godhead had given him to do. As he had revealed the character of his Father and devoted himself to the salvation of mankind, so they were to give themselves, however unworthy and insufficient, to the work of revelation and redemption.

*   *   *

Before they can recover from their hesitation and astonishment, a further step is taken. Jesus breathes on them, a symbolic act meaning that he is making them sharers of his life and power, his essential Spirit. The breath is the life: without breath we die, but with it we have energy and strength. So they have no need to be afraid. They can accomplish the divine mission because the divine breath or Spirit will be in them.

This commission carries with it a certain authority. In the name and in the power of God they are to face the moral evils of the world. The solemn phrase that has become familiar in the ordination of a priest has its meaning in relation to all God's disciples. The authority that, after our stumbling effort at penitence, bids us 'go in peace for the Lord hath put away your sins', is shared by the whole Church of God.

We realize this command afresh each Easter. The peace and power of the Resurrection make it impossible for the Church to remain a merely static body. We are a gigantic enterprise in which each member has his share. Before us lies the world in all its sin and misery, its false hopes and deluded joys. We are meant to advance upon it, to show it what God is really like and to win its members to his allegiance.

GOOD SHEPHERD

ANYONE who has had the good fortune to sit daily
at his study window looking over the Wiltshire
Downs, and to see the old shepherd, staff in hand and
dog at heel, leading his sheep to pasture, is in a favourable
position to understand the picture our Lord draws of
himself in Sunday's gospel.

The normal member of our industrialized society may
find himself less *en rapport* with the illustration, which was
drawn for members of a typically pastoral people.
Whether or not the Hebrews had produced the dynasty
of Shepherd Kings that once ruled in Egypt, they certainly had great shepherds among their patriarchs, and
David, their national hero, had learnt his trade as a
shepherd boy.

Perhaps it was the latter whom our Lord had in mind
when he said that it was characteristic of a good shepherd
to give his life for his sheep. David had faced the lion and
the bear: he had put his own person between his flock
and the threat of danger. So Jesus did; and after him
every true shepherd must give himself unsparingly for his
sheep. That he is the more likely to do if he 'knows his
sheep by name', that is, if he has a personal interest in
their individual lives. People respond to nothing so
readily as affection. If they know that we are interested
in them, they speedily become interested in us.

*   *   *

How different is the attitude of the typical hireling. To
him his work is just another job, a routine to be got
through. Having no personal interest in the concern, he

will work only according to rule. Even the better sort, who believe in properly earning one's wages, and take a professional pride in a job well done, when it comes to a question of hazard or danger or even more commonplace self-sacrifice, will still remember that this is not in the contract, and will shy at it like a horse refusing a jump.

What the hireling is really interested in, of course, is his wages. 'What is there in this for me?' That is a question that is almost certain to come into the minds not merely of the cynical, but even of the best of us, when some new call or opportunity arrives. Obviously, we cannot altogether disregard private interest: it would be hypocritical to profess to do so, and practically disastrous always to do so in effect. But what we can do, is by the grace of God to learn to put first things first; to regard the interest of the Master and the flock as paramount, and to set ourselves to serve that interest to the utmost of our power.

*   *   *

It is to the thought of the flock that Jesus turns after disposing of the shepherd and the hireling. And curiously, the one point he makes with regard to it is its comprehensiveness, a conception of which the obverse is its unity. The flock has been distributed among the various folds for the night. In the morning the shepherd makes his peculiar call, and his own sheep separate themselves from the rest and come out to make up his one flock.

Both simile and reality are a little unexpected. Jesus elsewhere has been so insistent that he was 'not sent except to the lost sheep of the house of Israel', and in spite of his kindness to the Syrophœnician woman, he was normally careful not to dissipate his energies among foreigners outside the borders of Israel. But St. John's gospel recognizes the universality of Jesus' appeal, and specially records his

interest when he was told that certain Greeks were
desiring to see him. There is evidently a proper missionary
application of the present text.

There is also an inescapable reference to what we
should nowadays describe as the 'ecumenical' theme.
God's final flock will be built up from many quarters.
But we must not confine the truth conveyed within purely
ecclesiastical limits. In a wildly distracted world, with
so many not knowing what spirit they are of or to what
master they belong, we must emphasize the notes of
unity, loyalty and authority even in the secular sphere.
The powers that be are ordained of God and need to be
drawn together as much as the *disjecta membra* of the Body
of Christ. So, as we are given grace, we may help to build
up the one flock of the one Shepherd, and by our faithful-
ness exhibit the unity both of the Church and the Kingdom.

BETWEEN THE ENDS

' A LITTLE while and ye shall not see me, and again a little while and ye shall see me.' There is what somebody has called a 'studied ambiguity' about our Lord's words which caused questioning in the minds of the disciples, as it does in ours today.

To what pair of events is he actually referring, to his Death and Resurrection or to his Ascension and his coming again? In all probability to both, because, although they are not identical in chronological order, yet they are strongly similar in their essential meaning, and that meaning can be best understood if the two pairs are held together.

It was important to Jesus that his followers should be prepared for his departure, but they must be made to realize that the separation would be fully consonant with an even closer 'union and communion' with him than they had enjoyed hitherto. Just as he would return to them on occasion after his Death, so he would return to them in perpetuity after his Ascension. They must realize that what they were concerned with was not a death but a birth, not a bereavement but a constantly expectant hope.

*   *   *

This was a salutary lesson for those for whom this gospel was originally written and who first heard it read. They were afflicted with a good deal of doubt. The Lord, whom they were expecting on the clouds of heaven, failed to appear. The dislike of their neighbours and the suspicions of the government were growing. What proof had they that he would come at all?

They had to learn that to live in faith without proof is the common lot of the Christian. They could be given no tangible, logical guarantee that their trust was not misplaced. It was therefore all the more comforting to hear the Lord preparing his disciples for just such a situation as that in which they now found themselves.

They were helped to realize what Christian life on this earth was always to be like, a living 'between the ends', one end already complete in the historical life of Jesus and the other still to come in the passing of this world and the institution of the 'world without end'.

They already enjoyed the invisible life of Christ through the Holy Spirit. That they must learn to hold on to without physical touch or sight. The belief that they already enjoyed the partial, but not complete, fulfilment of the promises of God would give them calmness in their present difficulties and confidence as they looked to the future.

*   *   *

This lesson we can certainly take to ourselves today. The line of demarcation between the Christian and the world grows sharper every year. The world now openly rejoices to be rid of Christ. Not only books and plays but many items on radio and television are permitted a freedom of denunciation that would have been unthinkable a generation ago. Violence of language and of crime seems constantly to increase. Even the young have learned to admit their addiction to drugs without any apparent sense of shame. In estimating the propriety of actions not only is one's obligation to others left out of count, but the possibility of a standard of morality and of a divine revelation is by many heroes of novels, stage and screen totally ignored.

Yet God has not left himself without witness. His goodness still manifests itself in many lives. Public helpfulness for the poor and distressed was never so great as it is today. Our youth can volunteer in ever greater numbers to serve backward or needy people in distant lands. A boy with a broken ankle can risk his life to rescue an unknown woman from a hotel fire. Such-like evidences abound that Christ still lives among his people. A little while and he will appear in glory to reign for ever.

THREEFOLD CONVICTION

THE work of the Holy Spirit is to convince men of the
saving truths of the gospel. And 'convince' in this
connection *means* convince: not just to win intellectual
assent, but to produce the kind of acceptance that results
in action.

The first conviction that he has to produce in us is
the unpalatable but fundamental truth of sin. Of a
universal tendency to wrong-doing he has no need to
convince us. All thinking men are aware of that already.
The psychologists and social scientists have left us in no
doubt of it today. But to convince us that when we act
wrongly we, generally speaking, act against God, and
that such wrong-doing is something for which we must
hold ourselves responsible: that is what the Holy Spirit
does. We cannot persist in taking refuge in the comfortable
suggestion that it is all due to heredity or to a bad
environment, and therefore is not our fault. We may distinguish as carefully as we can between freedom, responsibility and guilt, but in the last resort we must admit the
burden of sin.

And this need not be active wrongdoing. Perhaps most
sins are sins of omission. Not to believe in Christ, when
we have had ample opportunity to do so, is itself sin.
Goodness should appeal to goodness, faith to faith, spirit
to spirit; and if it fails to do so there must be something
wrong.

*   *   *

Happily there is another side to the picture. The Holy
Spirit does not only bring home to us the fact of sin; he

also convinces us of righteousness. It is not, after all, sin that is uppermost. In spite of all appearances to the contrary it is the right and not the wrong that has the last word in the affairs of man. Goodness still rules the world.

This truth is seen in the fact that in the long run Jesus himself was vindicated. If ever there had been an instance in which evil seemed to have triumphed over good, it was in his judicial murder. But he who had hung between two bandits was later received in triumph at God's right hand. The right ordering of things was made manifest to those who believed.

This conviction will lead men to continue in faith and hope even when they suffer the gravest injustice. If the Christian takes the most pessimistic view of man's situation in the present, he is at the same time most optimistic with regard to man's future. The hope of glory is as endemic in Christian life as the consciousness of sin. Because Christ goes to the Father and men see him with their physical eyes no more, they are confident that it is still love that makes the world go round.

*   *   *

There is a third point of which the Holy Spirit needs to bring conviction to our hearts, and that is that between the two conditions of sin and righteousness there must be a judgment. The world cannot be ruled under two flags: we cannot fight under two opposed banners. We must make up our minds to throw in our lot entirely with the one force or the other.

We are assured that there will be a final Judgment when the ultimate decision will be made: evil will be rooted out and the good will be established for ever. What is not quite so easy to realize is that the actual verdict has already been given. The Prince of this world has already been sentenced. Whatever may have been the case in pre-history, he was defeated by Jesus initially in the wilderness temptation and finally at the very moment when he seemed to have triumphed over Jesus in the Crucifixion.

It is on the side of that verdict that we must throw ourselves in utter conviction. We must recognize moral issues as paramount in our earthly life. Judgment begins with the household of God. We must judge ourselves now, lest we be adversely judged in the time to come.

In his heart everyone admires a *good* man. We must see that we follow the unique, the perfect example of that goodness in Christ.

PRAYER

'I WILL pray for you.' How often have we heard the
words said, and how often have they brought comfort
to us in our sorrow or our doubt. Yet there are those who
use them as a term of reproach as if they were the last
resource of one unable or unwilling to give any practical
help and anxious to escape from an embarrassing moment.

Jesus refrains from using them and explains why.
'I do not say I will pray for you. You have now been
brought into a new relation with the Father. You can
talk to him yourselves without the need for any inter-
mediary.' He is not decrying the practice of intercession.
He is rather emphasizing the fact that in this instance
intercession has reached its main objective and has
joined the persons prayed for with the Father.

Intercession, indeed, is the most valuable form of
prayer. It exercises the specific Christian virtue of *agape*,
consideration for others. It unites the Christian family
around the throne of God. It enables us to do something
for others when in fact there is nothing else we can do.
It sometimes opens up avenues of assistance which we
should not otherwise have found. It fulfils the command
to pray one for another. It is part of God's means for
the organization of his universe.

*　　　*　　　*

Prayer for others leads the way to prayer for oneself.
We need not be ashamed of praying for ourselves. In his
pattern prayer Jesus himself taught us to ask for the
satisfaction of our own needs both physical and spiritual.

Of course, we can only pray satisfactorily if we really

believe there is someone there who will listen. Clever
people, who are not quite certain how we can visualize
God, encourage us all the same to reflect how good a
psychological effect our prayers will have upon us by
smoothing out our troubled mind and bringing us to a
calm and reflective spirit.

But when I telephone to someone I am not much com-
forted by the mere act of dialling. Even when I hear the
double ring assuring me that I have got my number,
I am not much happier. It is not until I hear the familiar
voice answering me that I am really satisfied.

The cynic will point out that in prayer we never do
get that answering voice. But millions of faithful people
will rely on their own experience to prove the contrary.
Not always, perhaps, but often enough to assure us of its
reality, we have confidence that we have been in touch
with God.

*   *   *

Jesus told his disciples that henceforth they were to offer
their petitions in his name. In Hebrew thought the name
stood for the person. It does still even with us. 'Open, in
the King's name' (the phrase that sounded so thrilling
in our childhood's novels) means that the person who
makes the demand is at the moment standing for the
King, exercising his authority. If we are authorized to
pray in Christ's name, it is not just to add 'for his sake', but
to occupy his privileged position as the beloved child of
God who approaches his parent in the knowledge that his
request will be received with favour.

Our confidence is the greater because what we ask for
in the first instance is that God's own purposes may be
fulfilled. We are encouraged to think of God in the most
precisely personal terms. 'Our Father, hallowed be thy
name, thy kingdom come, thy will be done.' Astonishing

as it may seem, we are really praying for God himself. We are asking that he may be recognized throughout the world and all that he wants brought to pass.

This is indeed the beginning of all true prayer. It is a kind of meditation in itself. We put ourselves into the mind of God, resting in harmony with his thoughts, and only from that vantage-point do we turn to look out upon our own needs and those of others. We are one with the Giver of all good things, and so our petitions and intercessions cannot fail of true satisfaction.

GAZING UP

'WHY stand ye gazing up into heaven?' was the question asked of the disciples on the day that their Lord returned to his Father. It is the question once again asked by the new school of Cambridge theologians. But for rather different reasons.

The disciples were told in effect that Jesus was truly 'up there', but that they must get to work under the new conditions until he should come again and put an end to all earthly and temporal existence. We are being told today that we must think not of the God 'up there' or 'out there', but of the God within.

The two points of view are not necessarily contradictory: they only become so if one is emphasized to the exclusion of the other. Taken together, they are part of the paradox that lies at the very foundation of the Christian faith. God is both transcendent, external to the universe he has made, and also immanent within it, the source of the laws by which it has its being.

The teaching of the Ascension is a confirmation of this basic element of the Catholic faith. Christ, having finished his visible work on earth, inaugurated a new method of ministry by which, though resuming his immediate presence with his Father, he should be represented on earth in the hearts of his faithful followers by his Holy Spirit. The event in history is thus the confirmation of an eternal truth. If we hold fast to the event, we are more likely to keep the truth in proportion.

*   *   *

From the Ascension two results follow for each believer.

First he receives power, and then he becomes a witness.

How does he know that he receives power? Only by putting it to the test. We cannot be sure that we have power to keep ourselves swimming in the water until we have made the necessary movements with our arms and legs. We cannot be sure that we can ride a bicycle until we have had the courage and initiative to try to maintain our balance on the machine. So we cannot be sure that we have received the power of the Holy Spirit until we try to do something that requires reliance on that power.

The main purpose of this infusion of power is to make us consistent witnesses to Christ. Our lives, our thoughts, our words, our deeds must reveal our association with him. We must so live in him, be so saturated by the thought and love of him, that everything we do or say will reflect his influence. The missionary in a heathen society, the monk in his cloister, the man at the assembly line, the housewife in her kitchen, all alike must think, speak and act as if Christ's life were living in theirs— as indeed it is.

*   *   *

That is what the lovely Ascension collect means when it prays that 'we may also in heart and mind thither ascend, and with him continually dwell.' We are joined with him; therefore heaven is where we really live. As St. Paul tells us, our real status as citizens is in heaven. That is our place of origin and our real home. Here we are temporary visitors on a kind of passport. Similarly St. Augustine is for ever describing the Church on earth as a 'pilgrim' city: it is on its way back home. We too shall enjoy a kind of ascension when our work here is done.

The question is how to maintain our correct status in both worlds. Certainly not by forgetting our real home and behaving as if this world were all. Rather by making our surroundings here as reminiscent as possible of the eternal world to which we truly belong. It has often been observed that soldiers in temporary stations on campaign, and even prisoners when they have the opportunity, will set themselves to plant gardens, and make their environment as much like home as possible.

We can set about building a little heaven around us here, relying on the power of the Christ who has already returned to us in his Spirit. We can set about the task in complete confidence, knowing that he who has won the victory and enjoyed his triumph will make us more than conquerors.

SPIRIT OF TRUTH

THE truth, the whole truth, and nothing but the truth: that is what a trial in the courts is intended to elicit and what the judge tries to set before the jury in his summing-up. That kind of truth is a truth about actions and about the motives with which they were performed.

The scientist's idea of truth is something different. He is concerned about quantities, measurements, statistical relations; and he does not think he has got at the truth until he can express it in a mathematical formula. The artist's idea of truth is something different again. He has no use for evidence or for mathematics. He sees whether a picture is true to life by an inner light, a light that he may find it difficult to impart to other people. Indeed, as each man sees life from a different angle, he hardly expects his vision to be universally shared, as of course the judge and the scientist do.

When Jesus said 'I am the truth', he was thinking of truth in a way that included and at the same time transcended all these different conceptions. As is shown by the way in which he makes it the middle term between 'way' and 'life', he is thinking of truth as a personal matter, as a matter, if you will, of conduct and attitude, or better, as a matter of personal relationships. 'I am the true revelation of God who is all truth, the perfect expression of the right attitude to him, the complete example of the way of living in the light of his revelation.' And when Jesus says that his Spirit is the spirit of truth he means that the Spirit will make us see this clearly, and guide us into the best way of living our lives in the knowledge of that reality.

*   *   *

By living our lives after this fashion we shall ourselves become witnesses to the truth. We shall obviously have a standard of conduct, which the world as obviously lacks. Because we yield to that standard's authority and to it alone, we shall have a freedom which also the world lacks. 'Ye shall know the truth and the truth shall make you free.' Those who do not know it and have no clue to the fundamental truth of right relations to God have no more freedom than sheep without a shepherd or a dog without a master.

If the command to bear witness was addressed in the first instance to the apostles, because they had been with Christ 'from the beginning', it certainly applies also to every one of his followers. Indeed, it is only as each performs his own share of this allotted task that the Church can fulfil its vocation and prepare the way for the coming of the Kingdom. When one looks around at the generations that have been allowed to grow up in this country unevangelized ever since the Industrial Revolution, we cannot boast that we have performed our task very successfully. But the growing sense of mission on the part not only of clergy but laity encourages the hope that in future we shall be quicker to seize our opportunities. In this sharpening of our awareness we can see the work of the Spirit.

*   *   *

We are not to suppose that our witness will be made without difficulty. The greater part of Sunday's gospel is taken up with reminding us of the lions in our path. In some countries it is even still true that 'whosoever killeth you will think that he doth God service'—or the State or whatever passes to him for God. We in our more favoured lands must not expect our path to be entirely smooth. But the enduring of hardship is the way by which we work our passage home. We pray not to be led into temptation, yet, as the 'unknown' saying of Jesus has it, 'No man can obtain the kingdom of heaven that hath not passed through temptation.'

We may shrink as Jesus himself did. 'Let this cup pass from me.' Nevertheless, we can dare to add, paradoxical as it may seem, 'Not my will but thine', for we know that God will not allow us to be tried beyond our capacity successfully to resist. God never asks us to do more than he gives us power to do. And this power also is the gift of the Spirit of Truth, by which we are enabled to be true to ourselves and God.

THE REMEMBRANCER

Whitsunday *St. John* 14. 15

THE gospel for Whitsunday is admirably chosen: it
gives us a large part of the available information
about the Holy Spirit.

It was also admirably chosen by St. John to meet the
needs of his own day. If we ask why the fourth evangelist
picked on this particular episode from the conversation of
Jesus, the answer is clear. The people for whom he was
writing were second generation Christians. They had not
seen Jesus, nor had he yet appeared the second time.
How could they possess their souls in patience? By
meditating upon his immediate presence through his Holy
Spirit in their hearts, and listening to what Jesus said
about him.

They learn that he is the Spirit of Truth. He will
show them the really important things in life. In the
midst of much doubt and confusion he will enable them
to see clearly and choose their way in confidence.

In the old days he had spoken to and through the
prophets. He had enabled them to interpret aright the
history of their people. Where others had just seen a
secular series of cause and effect, they had been able to
discern the hand of God guiding the destinies of the
nations, and especially that of his own chosen people.
But now all the Lord's people were prophets, if they were
prepared to act as such; and they all through the Spirit
possessed the inner light by which they could discern
God's ways with men.

*   *   *

No doubt this is difficult to believe. We shrink from

claiming a specially privileged position. We do not like to set ourselves up as being different from our fellows. But, hard as it may be to realize, we *are* specially privileged. The Word has come to us: we have been baptized into Christ: to us were the promises made. . . . It is not that the Holy Spirit is not at work elsewhere. It is by his action that the whole universe is sustained in being. But he is not generally recognized.

The key to our special privilege is that we have had our eyes opened to the situation. If we deliberately close our eyes we can see nothing. The paradox of the work of the Holy Spirit is that he both arouses attention and responds to it. He will not give himself where there is no readiness to receive, but he will himself awaken the good intent. St. Paul could be called to attention even when he was on the way, full of zeal, to attack the followers of the Christ. The disciples were visited by the fire and the wind and were filled with ecstasy when they were waiting for they knew not what. The readiness is all.

*   *   *

In the City of London we have an exalted official whose title is The Remembrancer. His business, one presumes, is to keep the records and to see that everything runs smoothly in accordance with the traditions of the past. That must also involve, as in the case of the clerk in a magistrates' court, the giving of much advice as to the conduct of affairs in the present.

The task of the Spirit, we are told, is to be such a Remembrancer. He will 'bring all things to your remembrance, whatsoever I have said unto you'. The present generation of Christians could therefore be assured of the substantial truth of the record that the evangelists had handed on to them. The writers had felt themselves divinely helped to keep the record straight.

Willing acceptance of the gift of the Spirit by the new generation of Christians would do four things for them. It would bring them peace. They would be kept constantly in touch with the mind of Christ; and 'in his will is our peace'. Further, it would banish fear. They must not let their heart be troubled. Nor was there any call for them to be afraid, even in the midst of persecution, if Christ was, through his Spirit, so close to them.

Such confidence should deepen into actual joy. They were the lords of life: their leader held the throne over all the world: they had every reason for utter gladness. But above all, this new perceptiveness would strengthen their faith. They would not merely be accepting something external to themselves, in the sky or in the past, but they would be strengthened by their own experience. The Spirit would apply the truth to their own hearts, and it would become part and parcel of their own existence.

HEAVENLY THINGS

A POPULAR writer asked the other day why the clergy were so unwilling to preach on the subject of the Blessed Trinity. Granted that the underlying assumption is correct, which is more than doubtful, the obvious answer would be the difficulty of the subject. They would not wish to weary their hearers with abstruse arguments about a doctrine whose depths no man in this life can hope fully to plumb.

At the present moment, however, that hesitation, if it ever existed, has been swept away by the emergence of what is called the New Theology. This has embraced the deepest as well as the most superficial subjects and has made theologians of us all. The preacher who wishes to discourse on the subject of the Holy and Undivided Trinity has an audience ready made for him.

The representatives of the New Theology have attacked traditional teaching about God at two points, his transcendence and his personality. We should not picture God as outside and above his universe but within it: we should not emphasize his throne beyond the skies so much as his position as 'the ground of our being'. At the same time we should not talk so much about his personality as about the energy which is the subject-matter of scientific research. Instead of thinking of him as a father we should try to think of him as a great force or vital power animating the whole universe.

*   *   *

That, no doubt, is to put the situation crudely, and some of the leaders in the new movement have toned down their suggestions considerably. But, put thus baldly, the statement of the case enables us to see by contrast what is the precise force of the ancient doctrine of the Trinity. Indeed it might be said that the doctrine was actually framed in order to meet just such difficulties as are suggested here.

One of its main purposes is to maintain a correct balance between the ideas of God as above the world and within the world, between God as creator and God as the indwelling Spirit and sustainer of the universe. Indeed it does more: it preserves a third sphere in which God has operated, namely the stage of our own human history.

It is obvious that such a God, operating outside the universe, within it, and on the plane of history, must be a very different being from ourselves. Yet we *must* speak of him in terms of our own being, because that is the highest category that we actually know.

Consequently the doctrine of the Trinity says that God is personal but is more than *a* person. He is multi-personal, three persons in one God, Father, Son, and Holy Spirit.

*   *   *

Let us admit freely and gladly that this, which we believe has been made known to us by revelation, does not completely solve the mystery of God's being. If we could thoroughly understand his nature, then we should be as great as he is and he would no longer be God in the normally accepted meaning of the term. His ways are higher than our ways: he is vaster and more sublime than anything of which the human mind can conceive.

In all our thoughts on Trinity Sunday we must be content to preserve a wise agnosticism. We do not know all; but we believe firmly that God is more, and not less, than is implied in the precise phraseology of our creeds.

H

We can use the endearing terms that Jesus used of him and at the same time prostrate ourselves in utter adoration before his throne.

That, after all, is the purpose of the doctrine: not to give us something to argue about, but to move us to worship. The Book of Revelation finds the world of everyday reality too small to provide adequate pictures of the worship that is God's due, and ransacks the land of exalted dreams to add new glory to its acclamation of the divine majesty. If we, too, can ascend in heart and mind to that celestial sphere, we shall be able to bring some of its splendour into the life of every day.

RICH AND POOR

Trinity I   *St. Luke* 16. 19

TALES illustrating the sharp contrast between rich and
poor have been common in all lands and all ages,
and nowhere more than in the ancient East.

In our equalitarian society the contrast is not so obvious,
but where extreme poverty and extreme riches were to be
seen side by side there was every incentive for a story.
The contrast between Dives, who feasted not once in a
while but every day, and the beggar was a picture all too
familiar in our Lord's day.

There seems no suggestion that Dives was a particularly
bad man. He no doubt knew Lazarus by sight, as he
recognized him later. But he had never taken the trouble
to enquire into the causes of his condition or to relieve
his distress.

In other words, he was no worse than the average
German when he failed to take notice of what was going
on in Belsen or the average Englishman when he closes
his eyes to the conditions prevailing in some of our city
slums today. It is well, as far as we are concerned, that
television and the popular Press still find these conditions
a news-worthy story to tell.

*   *   *

Curiously enough the exchange of conditions on the
other side of the grave was also a not altogether un-
common element in the ancient story-teller's repertory.

What appears to be new in the parable is the change of
heart that Dives now manifests. For the first time in his
life he begins to think of someone else. True, the change
has not gone very far. Lazarus is still someone who can be

ordered about, and Dives' new-found charity does not
go beyond the limits of family pride. Yet one must always
begin somewhere, and it is significant as well as appropriate that Dives' first realization of the all-important
facts of life should drive him to think of his own brothers.

Family feeling was, and is, especially strong in the East,
but it prevails everywhere. Perhaps for that reason it is
in the family circle that it is most difficult to reveal a
change of heart. St. Francis of Assisi had to break with his
own family in order to follow the call of Christ. Bernard of
Clairvaux, on the other hand, drew his first followers into
austerity from among his own relatives. In any case we
are surely not meant to condemn Dives for not neglecting
his own family.

*　　　*　　　*

But here comes the difficulty for Dives. Was it not
already too late? The brothers have had the same opportunity as everyone else. They have the scriptures constantly
before them. Why should one suppose that they will heed
any fresh warning? Ah, but if someone went to them from
the dead! Surely they would be shaken out of their
complacency then.

Our Lord has no faith in the efficacy of portents. He
had shown that at the beginning of his ministry, when in
his temptation he refused to convert people by throwing
himself unharmed from the pinnacle of the temple. What
is wanted is a change of heart, and that is not the way to
procure it. Faith is not an unwilling acceptance of obvious
fact: it is the joyful allegiance of the whole personality.

It is easy to see why St. Luke chose this story for
insertion into his memoirs. He had always a strong feeling
for the poor, and there must have been many such in
his congregation. To them the Lord's vivid words must
have come with singular comfort. They were encouraged

to look forward to a time when their present disabilities would give place to a glory still to be revealed.

But also they were all evangelists: they were all engaged in the difficult task of converting the world. They no doubt often pined for some great cataclysm to prove the truth of their teaching and finish their work for them. But that was to pine for the impossible. Men are not converted that way. Christians must go on making their witness in their daily lives and speaking the word in season when opportunity serves. And they must then be content to leave the issue in God's hands.

FEAST OF LIFE

AS so often, Sunday's parable is the story of a feast.
A marked feature in Jewish expectation of a glorious
future was the Messianic banquet in which the faithful
would feed upon the carcase of Leviathan.

It is perhaps for this reason that Jesus chose the background of a feast for his parables. It would give them at
once a certain eschatological flavour: it would indicate
that he was looking towards the end, and was directing
attention to the Kingdom and to the choice that must be
made if one would enter into it.

But there is undoubtedly a wider significance. A teacher
could not go on using imagery of that kind without allowing it to reveal his main conception of life. He would not
so often in his lessons pick up the picture of a banquet, if
life did not habitually appear a pleasant thing. Jesus was
neither pessimist nor cynic. For him, in spite of all its
dangers and disappointments, its sufferings and sorrows,
life was a happy condition to be welcomed and enjoyed.

That is a point about which many people seem a good
deal less than certain. But it is quite fundamental to our
religion. Our Lord definitely reproaches those who take
the gloomier view. 'I came unto you eating and drinking,
and ye said "Behold a gluttonous man and a wine-bibber."
I piped unto you and ye did not dance.'

*   *   *

On what ground do people refuse to adopt this cheerful
outlook on life? Not, if the parable is to be accepted, from
any reason of outright antagonism. They are just too busy
to be bothered. Their own private concerns are much

more important to them than those of any neighbours.
They are satisfied with their own narrow horizons and
want no wider outlook. So any previous half-promise goes
by the board, and they send a merely formal refusal,
'regrets . . . cannot accept . . . previous engagement'. The
fact that a really handsome and expensive feast prepared
for their entertainment is likely to be wasted counts for
nothing at all.

No doubt the primary application of all this is to the
Jews' refusal to accept Christ's invitation to enjoy the full
pleasures of his Kingdom. But, as we have said, the wider
application is at least legitimate. It is also timely. The real
difficulty the Church of this generation encounters in its
mission is not opposition but apathy. The 'can't be
bothered: couldn't care less: so what?' attitude is all too
common. People are too engrossed in superficial pleasures
or mundane duties to listen to any serious invitation to a
fuller life, even though that life offers more genuine
satisfaction than they enjoy at the moment.

This is not wholly the fault of the Church. We are
sometimes told that if we were more zealous or put our
case more ably, the world would flock to listen. But there
is no guarantee of that. He who issued his invitation,
'Come unto me', in the most gracious words ever uttered
by man was not only rejected but crucified. Men's hearts
must be softened and their ears unstopped before they
will so much as listen, let alone respond.

*   *   *

However, the host does not suspend his efforts. There
were always some to whom one could turn, whether it
was the Gentiles in place of the Jews or the 'publicans and
sinners' in place of the avowedly religious section of the
nation. 'Compel them to come in.' One must not be afraid
to exert pressure (not physical force, as St. Augustine

thought, but the hospitable suasion that was thought to be good manners in the East).

We must not be surprised if it is the unexpected and the unlikely whom we finally see sitting at the feast. Every parish priest knows the wonder and the glory of it. Why did such and such an adult suddenly offer himself for baptism, for confirmation? Why do ordination candidates come from such improbable surroundings? The wind bloweth where it listeth, and (combining the scriptural metaphors) we must therefore sow beside all waters, not knowing where the seed will take root and germinate. And the best way of sowing this seed is to show that we ourselves fully appreciate and enjoy the feast of life to which we have been introduced in Christ, and of which the Eucharist, the great Thanksgiving, is the image and exemplar.

JOY IN HEAVEN

THE chapter of St. Luke from which Sunday's gospel is taken is often described as the very heart of the gospel. It does not merely, in Luke's characteristic style, emphasize God's love for sinners, but also in its three parables of restoration throws a tender and vivid light on the joy of heaven over 'one sinner that repenteth'.

The stories are told with exquisite artistry. It is therefore inevitable that we should look in them for some ascending scale of values. It is obvious that the final one, that of the Prodigal Son, is from every point of view a fitting climax to the whole; it is not so clear how the second, the Lost Coin, fits in. Dr. Clarke has suggested an implied contrast between the animal stupidity that causes the sheep to stray, the human carelessness that is responsible for the lost coin, and the deliberate choice that leads the prodigal into the wilderness of reckless living. Others have suggested that a special sentimental value attached to the lost coin, a silver drachma, because it was one of the chain of such coins worn by married women in the East. Its loss would be like that of a wedding ring to a modern European. The coin could therefore legitimately stand in the scale of human interest between the sheep and the son.

*   *   *

It is generally a mistake to look too closely into the details of parables. We are intended to concentrate on their main point. In each of these three cases the climax is the intensely human trait of impulsive, perhaps exaggerated, joy over the sudden recovery of some lost possession.

This homely touch is kept throughout. The owner of the sheep is so vitally concerned that he sets off in search of the stray himself. The woman sweeping her house as a last resort reminds us of the reassuring voice of a nurse or mother comforting the children who have lost some tiny treasure. 'Never mind, when we sweep we'll find it.' And then of course there is the excitement when what was lost is found. Everyone must know about it. We inevitably tell the first people we see, instinctively expecting them to share in our satisfaction.

Does it seem a little *naïve* to attribute such feelings to God? Would not his omniscience lead him to take a more balanced view and to have the whole situation in mind? Perhaps so, if we are determined to measure beauty with a foot-rule. But parables are not meant to be interpreted that way. We are taught to think of God in personal terms; and here is one of the most delightful emotions of which men are capable. We can thus think of God, who truly possesses all things, yet rejoicing over the recovery of something he had lost awhile.

*   *   *

The emphasis then is on the joy over the saved sinner. That joy is a social event. Even the court of heaven is depicted as thronged with a jubilant multitude. Everyone is expected to join in. Not until the third and culminating parable is it suggested that anyone can stand out, and then it is the returning delinquent's own brother. He, through jealousy, cynicism, and wounded pride actually shuts himself out of the heaven into which the prodigal has been received. So important a place does his defection occupy in the story that some have thought it must belong to a late appendix, while others, realizing its place in the whole, have wished to call the parable that of the Two Sons.

The evangelist tells us that the stories are aimed at the Pharisees, the self-righteous who don't like to see the outsider beginning to share their place in society. How often is the returning penitent cold-shouldered even in church!

In any case, whether the joy is social or not, it is over the single repentant sinner. That is a salutary lesson in the age of collective man, when everywhere, in school, in factory, in union, in Parliament itself, immense pressure is brought to bear upon the individual to merge himself in the mass. Yet it is as individuals that we are born, as individuals that we die; it is only as individuals that we can be converted. We can only give our own heart to Christ and not another's. Happy are those who have the gift of individual affection through which they can lead the seekers one by one to Christ.

RULE OF LIFE

SUNDAY'S gospel is taken from St. Luke's 'Sermon on the Plain', which corresponds to St. Matthew's better-known 'Sermon on the Mount'.

It is perhaps a pity that the title 'sermon' has been given to either of them, for they are not carefully constructed, logical exhortations such as are generally known by that name. They are more like what we should now characterize as 'tabletalk'—collections of sayings uttered at different times by a beloved teacher and carefully collected and recorded by his hearers.

Nevertheless it is sometimes possible to discern or imagine a connected sequence of thought in these compositions. In Sunday's extract, which deals with the rule of life for a Christian, we can see successive emphasis on the attitude, the aim and the means.

The attitude is simple: be merciful. The follower of Christ must not be censorious; he must not be quick to judge his fellows. He must always be ready to give another the benefit of the doubt. He must get rid of the habit of thought that takes it for granted that everything and everybody in our surroundings are wrong.

*   *   *

What is our aim in all this so far as our own interior life is concerned? It is nothing less than perfection. That does not mean an immediate point beyond which no further progress can be made. The American translation for the word rendered 'perfect' is 'fully taught', and others might render it 'completely initiated'. It implies a mature and adult condition in which our feet are set on the right road of development and along which we can continue to progress—rather like a flower which is perfect in the bud but still has to develop its full quality.

It is only as we have this aim that we dare to offer leadership to others. We must have some standard of judgment, because, however much we are determined to avoid being censorious, we must not shrink in the last resort from deciding between good and bad, right and wrong. If we cannot see the goal ahead ourselves, we are like one blind man offering to lead another: any unexpected obstacle will trip us both.

If we are in doubt, we have one sure guide, and that is to follow our Master. There is perfection in him and we shall always be pursuing it if we follow in his footsteps. We can learn to translate the example he set into the terms of our own everyday life. We may make mistakes, but, if we act in good faith, even they will be remedied in the long run and their consequences turned to good.

*   *   *

It follows that the means by which we can keep this aim steadily before us and maintain a truly 'merciful' attitude towards others is by thoroughly knowing ourselves. If we are blind to our own character we shall certainly be blind to the true character of everyone else. We cannot hope to remove a speck of dust from another's eye, if we have a great log or beam protruding from our own.

If then we are quick to recognize others' faults, we must reflect that our own, given the advantages of our situation, are probably much worse. In any case we should not be so ready to recognize faults in others and to offer gratuitous advice for their removal. People who live in glass houses should not throw stones. The pot should not call the kettle black. The very multiplication of such proverbs shows how common is this particular kind of hypocrisy.

We can avoid it only by recognizing our own frailty. Here lies one of the remedies of our Christian religion. Most other philosophies and ethical systems are devoted to boosting a man's ego, making him realize how great a person he is, and giving him confidence in himself.

The Christian faith tells us we must begin by recognizing that we are nothing. We come to God as little children, weak and having nothing of our own. He fills our hands and our hearts, and gives us the power to achieve the aim he has set before us. It is only when we realize that our sufficiency is of God that we are truly set on the way of perfection.

CASUAL TURNING-POINT

IT is always fascinating to learn how another man
received the impetus that set him on his course for
life, to discover what made him follow this or that calling,
what gave him his particular attitude to the world, and his
special place in its history.

Sunday's gospel tells us what was the turning point for
Peter. He received his life's direction from a seemingly
casual incident at the Lake of Galilee. We are not sure
whether it was the first time he had met Jesus, for we are
told by St. Luke that Jesus had already been to his home
and healed his mother-in-law. In any case it seemed more
or less by accident that Jesus ran across him with his part-
ners mending and drying their nets after a fruitless night's
fishing.

It so happened that the crowds were thronging round
Jesus and that he was looking for some sort of rostrum
from which he could address them more conveniently.
So he suggested that Peter should shove his boat a little off
shore so that he could use it as an improvised pulpit. It
must have been a nuisance to Peter, who would rather
have finished his work and gone home to bed. But with
his usual good nature, and perhaps remembering the
kind deed done to his wife's mother, he tossed his net into
the boat, held it steady for Jesus to get in, and shoved off.

It is extraordinary how often a casual event, a chance
salutation, an easy kindness to a stranger may change a
whole life. In this age it changed not an individual life
only but the history of the Church, and so of the world.

*   *   *

Of course nothing of importance might have happened if the incident had just ended there. Not even Jesus' sermon seems to have made any noteworthy impression. But the fact is that, when Jesus, wishing to do Peter a good turn, told him to renew his efforts for a catch, he did as he was told, although he could not refrain from a little grumbling. This time the exercise of good nature resulted in a tremendous haul of fish.

This scene seems to have struck mediæval Churchmen with extraordinary force. It appealed to them on two levels. They were so many of them fishermen of a sort themselves that they could never forget the picture of the big catch. But the narrative seemed too good to be left just on that level. And so they added an allegorical explanation making the fisherman Christ and his net the Church, while the sea was the world, and the fish the rescued souls.

The point of this was that in the heyday of evangelism so many converts were won that the ecclesiastical organization was not able to cope with them, and the machinery broke down. Or more subtly still, the influx of barbarians was so great that it seemed likely that they might overwhelm the whole cultural structure of the Christian life.

*　　　*　　　*

To Peter himself the totally unexpected success of the manœuvre came as a great shock, and not altogether a pleasant one. His dominant emotion was fear. The man who could effect such a reversal of fortune must be more than human. He must belong in some way to the supernatural sphere. Contact with the powers of the other world might easily be dangerous, particularly if one's life was not above reproach. Conscience doth make cowards of us all. So Peter's reaction was one of revulsion. 'Depart from me, for I am a sinful man, O Lord.'

Jesus' answer is to tell him not to be afraid. To that is added the half-punning suggestion: 'Don't worry; you will soon be catching something better than fish.'

Peter and his companions only waited to beach their boats and then immediately set out on their career as followers of Jesus. That career was to involve for some of them not only hardship, sorrow, and physical torture but actual martyrdom. But through it all ran the joy of serving the Master they loved, and so of gaining confidence in the ultimate victory of their cause.

MORAL URGENCY

WE hear a good deal today about the New Morality. It is refreshing to turn back to the time when Christian morality really was new. Sunday's gospel, with its excerpt from the Sermon on the Mount, gives us a good idea of its first proclamation.

Jesus takes for granted that a change was needed. The Scribes and Pharisees were accepted as representatives of the old standard, and 'unless your righteousness shall exceed the righteousness of the Scribes and Pharisees, ye shall in no case enter into the Kingdom of Heaven.'

Where they had gone wrong was in allowing their first piety to be replaced by legalism. Through adhering too rigidly to a code they had submerged their first simplicity and affection under a load of anxiety. They had become harsh to all who were not capable of their strict religiosity, and over-scrupulous in respect of themselves and their own conscience. The love and joy that should be the keynotes of true religion had been replaced by fear. And fear had led them to keep up appearances, even when they failed in performance. Jesus did not shrink from calling them hypocrites.

*   *   *

The change came when Jesus recalled them to the original intent and meaning of the law. As the Messiah proclaiming, like John the Baptist before him, the characteristic morality of the Kingdom, he is not afraid to sweep aside all the heaped-up ingenuity of rabbinic argument, and to get back to first principles. 'It was said by them of old time . . . but I say unto you.'

Jesus did not abrogate the old law: he told his hearers that they must go beyond it. He fulfilled the law by asking people to live it out not only in the letter but in the spirit.

What was important in the first place was not the act but the motive. The essential point to attack was not the end but the beginning, not the finished product in the deed but the first inception of the thought when desire moved towards it.

To bring home the lesson Jesus gives an example. Murder is an act definitely forbidden in the Mosaic Law. But where does murder begin? In the anger felt in the heart and the fury so often expressed in bitter words. These emotions are not, and cannot be, regulated by law, but in the eyes of God they are as reprehensible as the act to which they lead.

*   *   *

It was not Jesus' habit to denounce faults without suggesting a remedy. He does not take the common way out by implying that things may not be so bad after all and that perhaps God will be lenient. He maintains the severity even of the new law against sin, but he points a way by which we may avoid the temptation itself. The best way not to experience anger against others is to see that they have no cause to be angry with you.

This was said at a time when the followers of Jesus were still attending services in the temple at Jerusalem. He uses the fact to provide an illustration of his meaning. If you are taking a sacrificial gift to the temple and are actually at the point of handing it over to the priest at the altar and then you suddenly remember that you have done someone a wrong, then leave your gift without waiting to see it offered. Go and put the wrong right, and then come and complete your offering.

Nothing could be more graphic or emphasize more

strongly the need for urgency in the moral life. The rectification of sin brooks no delay. We must not, if we can avoid it, allow ourselves to be overtaken in a fault. It is a matter of prudence to correct a situation before it goes too far and gets out of hand. Particularly is this true in regard to personal relations. Reconciliation is the keynote of the Christian law.

NOTHING TO EAT?

THE feeding of the four thousand was due to the Lord's compassion. Not many of his miracles are ascribed to this motive.

Some were answers to faith, some were signs that the Kingdom had begun, some were manifestations of power, some were just wonderful works. Perhaps the evangelists felt the awkwardness of the question, 'If compassion was the normal motive, why were they not universal—to meet every need?' But that of course would have implied an entirely different kind of universe from that in which we live.

Here the question hardly arose. It was a particular, isolated, situation. Those who had followed Jesus, fascinated by his teaching and engrossed in his words, had come out inadequately provided. They had almost exhausted their meagre supplies. It was now the third day since they had set out; they were hungry. Jesus, himself perhaps hungry too, feels with them. He saw their immediate need and had compassion on them.

St. Mark was telling this story for a Christian congregation. There is no doubt about the inference they would draw. They too had been hungry, hungry in soul if not in body. They had realized the emptiness of life as presented to them in their contemporary world. In all that great wilderness they could find no satisfaction, not in the power of Rome, in the religiosity of the mystery cults, or in the factiousness of Judaism. They had looked to Jesus; he had had compassion on them, and supplied their need.

*   *   *

Nor can we doubt how they would interpret what followed. Jesus had called for such supplies as remained; he had received them, said grace in the customary manner, broken one of the thin round loaves, and passed the food to his disciples for distribution among the crowd. And the supply had not failed.

There is a ritual quality about the narrative which must strike us today with nearly as much force as it did its original hearers. The evangelist is using words and phrases which deliberately evoke, as a parallel to the miracle, a scene that was regularly enacted in the midst of the congregation. 'He took, he blessed, be broke, he gave . . .' what are these but the actions of the celebrant at every Eucharist?

And so the listeners in the Christian synagogue would remember how Christ regularly met their need in the Holy Communion when the presiding elder, acting in his name took, blessed, broke, and gave the bread they themselves had brought for the purpose. This connection between miracle and Communion became so rooted in their thoughts that the picture of a basket containing loaves and fishes is one of the earliest and commonest representations of the sacrament in Christian art.

*   *   *

'So they did all eat and were filled.' There is a note of satisfaction and gratitude here which is equally appropriate for the beneficiaries of the miracle and for the Christian congregation. To 'return thanks' after meals, as after Communion, keeps us in touch with the Giver of all good things and reminds us that even the satisfaction of our temporal needs comes from the eternal.

But why the mention of the seven baskets? Is it merely to point a contrast with the feeding of the five thousand; or is it to emphasize the greatness of the miracle; or is it to rebuke possible wastefulness; or is it a mere casual relation of what actually happened? There must, one thinks, be some purpose in it. And what better purpose could there be than to underline the generosity with which God meets our needs? In Christ's provision it is never true that 'the hungry sheep look up and are not fed'. Whether in the Palestinian hills or in the Christian congregation those who look up to him receive enough and to spare. Always he has compassion on the multitude, and his bounty is inexhaustible. 'He feels his heart moved' by the consciousness of their need, and out of the stirring of his pity come abundant supplies for our profit.

THE TEST OF A PROPHET

JESUS was not in the habit of addressing the air. He always spoke to the immediate condition of his hearers. When he gave a warning, it was of some real and not merely fanciful danger.

We need to remember this when we read or hear the unexpected command: Beware of false prophets. We know that there were such people in Old Testament times. They had brought an unwholesome touch of professionalism into the preacher's office and they had replaced the gift of the Spirit with a blind nationalism. Their preaching was dictated less by the Word of God than by self-seeking motives. It was well to beware of them.

But were there such persons in Jesus' own time? We know that there was a revival of prophecy in contemporary Judaism, as is evidenced by the work of John the Baptist. It is possible that some of the false Messiahs of the period also presented themselves in the guise of prophets. We know, too, that there were many Christian prophets and that St. Paul rated the gift of prophecy very highly.

Among the Christian prophets there were certainly some who exercised the gift from unworthy motives. When the best is corrupted the worst may be expected. The knowledge of unusual gifts may become a temptation to acquire wealth or power. Browning's Mr. Sludge, the medium, was honest enough to begin with, but in the end he became a mean and hypocritical villain.

*   *   *

In such circumstances it becomes necessary to have some standard of judgment, some criterion by which one can distinguish good from bad. In the Old Testament a quite simple test was proposed: if what the prophet says comes to pass, he is a true prophet; if it does not, he is false. The difficulty there was that too often by the time you had your answer the need for it was gone.

In one of our earliest Christian documents a different test was proposed. If a prophet, allegedly speaking in the Spirit, ordered an *agape*, a public banquet, and then partook of it himself, he was a false prophet. The remedy there was quaint: not to allow any prophet to share in a charity feast that he had ordered himself, and so to ensure his disinterestedness.

Besides these plain but limited expedients Jesus' own test seems profound and universal. 'By their fruits ye shall know them.' It was the test he was anxious people should apply in his own case. When his critics doubted him he invited them to look into his life and see whether his deeds and his general manner of conducting himself did not support his claims.

Today we are inclined to disparage moral judgment, and to value tolerance above all the virtues. Certainly no one wants to be censorious. But we have a definite duty to ourselves and to others to distinguish between good and evil. Tolerance can itself become a vice.

*   *   *

To Jesus' warning there is added a short appendix defining the nature of true religion. Not everyone who says the creed and joins in public worship is received into the Kingdom of Heaven, but only those who obediently do God's will. The important thing is not the God on the lips but the God in the heart.

Even the best of us may find on close examination that the aims he is really pursuing are quite different from the ones he is professing. The preacher may be admiring his own eloquence while affirming the long-suffering of God. The theologian may be seeking fame while expounding the nature of the Trinity. The churchwarden's real God may be in his account-book: the housewife's in her beautifully kept home.

What we must make sure of is our ruling passion. God must be allowed to set up his throne in the heart. His presence there will ensure our sincerity: we shall then no longer be afraid to acknowledge that in the long run the tree can be recognized by its fruits.

PRUDENCE

ONE is inclined to wonder whether it was lack of humour or just sympathy with those of us who are hard of understanding that caused the revisers of 1928 to give us an alternative gospel for Trinity IX.

Certainly the parable of the Unjust Steward has often been found difficult, and its humour is of a kind that is more common in the East than among ourselves. In the steward's company we think of the Thief of Baghdad and a host of clever rascals who have been the central figures of Oriental tales. In any case we miss the real point of the parable if we do not put it in that category. It is a story intended to show to what lengths a clever but unscrupulous man will go in order to ensure his safety and comfort. We are intended to realize in sharp contrast how very careless ordinary people can be in ensuring their eternal welfare.

After all, the steward is a man of great enterprise and resource. When he is on the point of losing his job, he takes steps to bring his neighbours under obligation to him. He will not shrink from a little blackmail.

The master, in true Eastern story fashion, makes no comment on his servant's lack of morality. He is simply amused at the cleverness of the tactics employed. The inference is that we are to be equally clever and painstaking over the things that really matter.

*   *   *

The parable is essentially a lesson in what the moralists call prudence, one of the four cardinal virtues. It deals with prudence both in its general meaning and also in its special application to money.

In modern society we are not in the habit of making much of the virtue of prudence. No doubt parents commend it to their children in the privacy of the home, but in public we are much more likely to extol the adventurous and even the reckless spirit. After all, the deeds of derring-do make much more exciting reading in the headlines and the novels.

Nevertheless the more homely virtue of prudence *is* one of the cardinal virtues, without which no life can be successfully lived. Indeed, without it no life could even last: we have to protect ourselves against dangers every day. We must not be misled into interpreting the text, 'Take no thought for the morrow', as if it were a licence for sheer carelessness. The New English Bible translates, 'Do not be anxious about to-morrow.' Prudence comes between carelessness and anxiety.

It follows with immense force that, if prudence about everyday matters is so commendable, we have no right to be careless about the things that concern eternal welfare.

*   *   *

The special implication of the parable is the need for prudence in the use of money. 'Make for yourselves friends by means of the mammon of unrighteousness.' The word mammon simply means money. It is the 'unrighteous' mammon because in itself it is outside the sphere of morality: it becomes good or bad merely as we use it well or ill.

Our forebears thought much more of the virtue of thrift than we do. In the comfortable surroundings of the Welfare State we are often encouraged to live up to the total of our income without any thought of saving for a rainy day. This is bad advice, even for our own security and peace of mind. It is worse if it removes from our hearts the desire to do the best we can for our children or others for whom we have some responsibility.

The money handled by the wily steward was not his own. The current Christian stewardship campaigns have taught many of us that we too hold what we have in trust for the service of God and our fellow-men. We shall not deal with it selfishly or recklessly. We shall not copy the spendthrift or the gambler. We shall use such money as we have in order to make a home for ourselves in the hearts of those whom we have the privilege of helping, and in the eternal mansions where dwells the Master to whom we must one day give account.

THE TEACHER'S TEARS

THE sight of Jesus weeping over the doomed city is a revealing picture of the love of God as contrasted with the thoughtlessness of men. It may have been the suddenness with which the scene burst on his view, at the turn of the road in that long descent into Jerusalem, that overwhelmed him with the swift protective sense of a parent for a helpless child. The sharp revelation of its 'cloud-capped towers, gorgeous palaces', some scarcely yet completed, yet all alike soon to be left a crumbling heap, was too much for his emotions.

He wept over the city, as any humanitarian would who realized the loss its destruction would involve not only to art and culture, but to human life and progress. He wept over it as a patriot who realized that this might mean the end of his people with their distinctive way of life. He wept over it as a prophet who had done everything possible to warn God's chosen race of their impending judgment. He wept over it as the Redeemer who had come to save his people from their sins, and who even in face of their defiance was still prepared to continue the effort even at the cost of his own life.

If only they had known! But they were self-blinded. They could not, or would not, recognize the critical nature of the times or their own moral responsibility. They knew not the time of their visitation.

*   *   *

Perhaps the cleansing of the Temple is best looked upon as a last effort to shake them out of their lethargy and to stab them broad awake. What ordinary teaching could not do, some swift prophetic action might succeed in doing. All were familiar from their schooldays with the way in which the prophets of old had reinforced their sermons with dramatic effect. The horns of iron made by Zedekiah to push the Syrians, the yokes first of wood and then of iron that Jeremiah could wear to foretell foreign domination, the rending of the new garment to represent the division of the people, all these and many others were acted parables intended to drive home the point of the teacher. Nay more, in some mysterious way they were expected actually to influence the event they portrayed. The cleansing of the Temple was a 'sign' that judgment was already beginning at the very heart of the nation.

Does not God still deal with us after the same fashion? Some cataclysmic happening that halts the even flow of our careless lives is not just a manifestation of frightening powers outside our control. However natural may be the immediate cause, it is intended by God to startle us out of our apathy and to make us take stock of our situation in his eyes. As the cleansing of the Temple was undoubtedly intended to be reflected in the moral cleansing of the nation, so the unusual happening, even in the individual life, is expected to open our eyes to the true purpose of our probation here on earth.

*   *   *

But it is not by the unusual or the dramatic alone that God acts. He teaches us in the events of every day. We must not expect always to be bludgeoned into belief by the unexpected occurrence, by the thunder-bolt out of a blue sky. 'If they believe not Moses and the prophets, neither will they be persuaded though one rose from the dead.' Therefore after his eviction of the merchants and moneychangers from the Temple, Jesus resumed his normal function as a teacher.

It is this daily teaching that is the regular sustenance of our lives. As the steady alternation of night and day, summer and winter is sufficient for the perfect revelation of natural beauty, so the ordinary course of human existence should be enough to reveal to us the ways of God with man. 'The daily round, the common task will furnish all we need to ask.' If our eyes were open, we could not fail to see it. But few things are more difficult than to attain this condition of constant awareness. ' 'Tis we, 'tis our estranged faces that miss the many-splendoured thing.' We need to pray that God will turn our faces to him, that he will open our eyes and keep them riveted upon him. So only shall we spare our divine Teacher his tears.

THE SUPERIOR PERSON

SUPERIORITY is the most devastating of all the milder faults of disposition. Just because it does not flame out like anger, hatred or malice, but worms its way unobserved into the mind, it can corrupt a whole nature and ruin all our intercourse with our fellow-men before it is recognized for what it is. White ants can eat out all the interior of a beam of wood leaving it apparently intact, and the damage is only discovered when some weight is placed upon the empty shell. The Christian soul can be 'white-anted' by the simple urge to feel superior.

Superiority makes us look down upon our neighbour and forget our own faults. The feeling may arise from considerations of birth, wealth, position, talents or even looks. However it comes, it helps us to feel that we are on a higher level than others, and can speak to them *de haut en bas*. It may, of course, be a defence mechanism. But whatever its cause, it is a complete negation of the method of the Incarnation. God became man precisely in order that he might stand on the same level with his creatures.

*   *   *

All this is pictorialized for us in the unforgettable story of the Pharisee and the Publican. The Pharisee was a religious leader. He belonged to the class to whom the Jews owed most of their progressive ideas. He and his fellows had brought religion out of the temple and the synagogue and translated it into the terms of everyday life. They had done much more: they had peopled the unseen world with spirits and penetrated the secret of a life beyond the grave. They possessed all the ingredients of a live religion, knitting the affairs of every day with the eternal and the infinite. The trouble was that the Pharisee thought he was somehow earning all these privileges for himself. 'I fast twice in the week, I give tithes of all that I possess.' So he could naturally look down with contempt on 'the lesser breeds without the law'.

By contrast the Publican knew himself a worm. He was so recognized by the society in which he moved. He was a thorough Quisling: he was collecting taxes from his own people on behalf of a hated foreign power. He was probably enriching himself in the process. If any ego needed a defence mechanism, it was surely his. Yet he does not create one. He does not even begin to compare himself with his fellows, as the Pharisee did. He only sees his own sordidness against the white holiness of God, and the consequent judgment of his own conscience overwhelms him. 'God be merciful to me a sinner.'

*   *   *

We have in the New Testament one illustrious and illuminating example of a man who changed from one condition to the other. Paul was once a Pharisee of the Pharisees. He was among the foremost in their ranks. He was a whole-hearted, indeed a fanatical, observer of the law. No one valued the traditions and privileges of his people more highly than he. To be so called out and favoured by God was worth a lifetime of devoted service. And Paul tried hard to earn his salvation, to render adequate payment for it in the meticulous performance of religious duties. 'I fast twice in the week', he might have said; 'I give tithes of all that I possess.' In the result he found himself hard, unhappy, superior to his neighbours but conscious of utter failure in the sight of God.

And then came the experience on the Damascus road.

He realized with appalling clarity the utter worthlessness
of the case he had been building up for himself. At one
fell blow he lost his old faith, his position, his career,
his store of merit, everything. And in that moment of
complete annihilation, Jesus offered him salvation as a
gift, without payment, without desert. And the proudest
Pharisee of them all became the humblest Publican.
'God be merciful to me a sinner.' 'Lord, what wouldst
thou have me to do?' No wonder that ever after Paul
taught that the very essence of the gospel is to accept
salvation as a free gift, realizing that we can never earn or
deserve it. No wonder that ever after the worst of all sins
seemed to him pride, or what in modern English we
should call superiority.

THE MIRACLE

NOW that we have come to see that some at least of our gospels were originally written to be read as 'lessons' in church, it is natural that we should ask of any passage, 'What did the evangelist intend to teach the congregation by this?'

It adds a new dimension to our study of the scriptures. We want to know, not only the significance of any event in itself, but also the reason why the author selected it out of all the material at his disposal and drew the special attention of his readers or hearers to it. In fact we treat each individual passage very much as we would treat a story told us in the pulpit today. We inevitably think not only of the intrinsic value of the narrative but of the preacher's point in telling it.

Judged by this standard, there can be little doubt why St. Mark narrated the healing of the deaf mute. (It is more difficult to understand why the other evangelists did not follow him and narrate it too.) His congregation was of the second generation of Christians. He wanted them first to have the most vivid knowledge he could produce of the way in which Jesus went about doing good, and then he wanted to arouse in them the same feeling of adoring praise as the miracle had induced in the original eye-witnesses.

*   *   *

A feature that is particularly noticeable in this narrative is the detailed way in which it is recorded. Granted that Mark always had a journalist's eye for detail and would probably produce a vivid narrative anyway, there seems some particular reason for the careful enumeration of the steps taken in this case—the leading aside, the touch of the fingers, the use of saliva, the calling upon heaven, the 'sighing' or heavy breath. Why all these details?

One can only suggest that it is in order to let the congregation know that Jesus was accustomed to do just what the people would expect a healer to do. We know from the offended tone of Naaman's remarks about Elisha in 2 *Kings* 5, that there was an established custom in these matters, just as there is, no doubt, among our own healers today. Certainly it was Jesus' own custom, wherever possible, to follow common practice and so to associate himself as closely as possible with his neighbours. Thus it was common form to suppose that power was conveyed by touch, by spittle, or by breath.

There was, however, one striking difference. When the cure had been effected, Jesus disclaimed all credit for himself. By implication he also dismissed any possible suggestion of magic. Normally Jesus openly gave all the credit to faith, either the patient's or his friends'. Here not even that is mentioned, and the only indication of the source of the healing is to be seen in the upward glance to heaven.

*   *   *

Of course, this disposes of the old idea that Jesus performed his miracles in order to 'prove his divinity'. It is doubtful whether any miracles could ever prove divinity, and it is certain in any case that Jesus did not want that kind of proof. He did not wish to bludgeon people into unwilling assent: he desired faith; that is, deliberate personal allegiance.

Nor can it be said that the main purpose of the miracles, even those of healing, was to show compassion. It is no doubt true that he did in point of fact manifest compassion: it would be quite incredible that he could ever see suffering without feeling sorrow for the sufferer. But if that had been the main impulse of the miracles, it would have demanded similar relief for *all* sufferers, and that would have required a new plan for the universe.

It seems most likely that the miracles were intended to serve as part of the proclamation of the gospel—the news that the Kingdom of God had come. In this case the present miracle was singularly appropriate. Isaiah had long ago announced that in the Messianic Kingdom the ears of the deaf would be unstopped and the tongue of the dumb would sing for joy.

The knowledge that the prophecy had been fulfilled was too much for the eye-witnesses. They couldn't keep it to themselves. The first words the deaf man hear were the loud and repeated praises of God. May they echo also in our own hearts.

ETERNAL LIFE

SUNDAY'S gospel follows hard upon the famous 'Johannine' passage in St. Luke which is the high-water mark of Jesus' claim for himself. 'All things have been delivered to me by my Father; and no one knows who the Son is except the Father, or who the Father is except the Son and he to whom the Son is willing to reveal him.'

This saying itself has arisen out of the successful mission of the Seventy, and Jesus has thanked his Father for making simple folk the recipients of this revelation of his power. He now turns to his disciples and congratulates them privately on their good fortune in being allowed to see what so many great people in Church and State have longed to see, the glories of the Messianic Kingdom.

No doubt the disciples needed to be reminded how favoured they were. It was not easy for them to recognize the Messiah in the carpenter's son nor the unique character of the miracles of the Kingdom in a wonder-loving age. It is very hard for any of us fully to recognize the special value of our times. It needs the particular genius of the poet to shock us into realization, and then we think that he exaggerates and talk rather condescendingly of 'poetic licence'. But here there was something quite particular and special: the eternal had entered after a new fashion into time. A new age had been inaugurated, and it was proper that the disciples should recognize its unique character to the full.

*   *   *

It may have been this incident that prompted the

question of the lawyer, or at any rate brought it to the mind of the evangelist. 'How shall I enter this state of bliss? I know the Kingdom is not just a question of diplomacy and armed forces. It is a state of life, life lived in a new dimension, eternal life. How then can I make sure of it? Like a wise teacher, our Lord leads him to answer himself. The summary of the law, in which he had been brought up from childhood, could not be bettered. Love God and your neighbour and you are already in that higher state of existence: you already have eternal life.

The two loves, of course, are not precisely identical, though they may grow out of each other. The love of God is from the lower to the higher. It is passionate adoration, fervent worship, humble aspiration. The love of one's neighbour is from equal to equal. It is sympathy, compassion, the determination to serve his highest interests even at real cost to oneself. There is no emphasis, as has been suggested, on the 'as', implying that we are to love our neighbour just as much as, and no more than, we love ourselves. Indeed, St. Paul has already passed that limit when he puts the neighbour's interest in front of one's own: 'in honour preferring one another'.

*   *   *

But the summary of the law was too tame for the lawyer. It was familiar to the point of boredom. So he takes the usual way of escape for those unwilling to face main issues. He runs out on a technicality. 'Who precisely is my neighbour?' Jesus, however, allows him no such evasion. He does not discuss the question. He does something much more important. He tells him how one can be neighbourly. And he drives the point home in a very characteristic and unforgettable story.

The Good Samaritan showed himself neighbourly. The priest and levite no doubt excused themselves on just such a technicality as the lawyer had raised. The man was no acquaintance of theirs; they did not want to get mixed up in anything; and they had a duty not to risk defilement. So they passed by on the other side. The despised Samaritan, however, just saw a human need and went straightway to meet it. And in doing so he showed himself a member of the Kingdom.

Simple, isn't it? Do you want to be sure of the Kingdom? Then show yourself friendly. Not fussy, but just friendly. Are you a friendly person? Then by so much you already enjoy the blessings of the Kingdom and of eternal life.

COURTESY

Trinity XIV   *St. Luke* 17. 11

ADVERSITY makes strange bed-fellows. So runs the proverb, and we see it exemplified almost every day.

People who normally would avoid each other, when they are faced by some common calamity will forget their mutual animosity and seek protection in each other's company. That is true in many cases of earthquake, fire and flood. It is equally true in the less spectacular cases of politics and industrial trouble. It is in fact one of the few remaining hopes for British industry today.

At any rate it was true of the ten lepers in the gospel story. Their little band included a Samaritan, a man of hated race whom the Jews persisted in calling a foreigner and to whom in normal circumstances they would not even have spoken.

Now, however, driven out from the haunts of men and obliged to render each other the common services of humanity, even perhaps on occasion to prey upon the more fortunate members of society, the Jewish sufferers could tolerate the presence of the despised foreigner in their midst. It is one of the most valuable lessons of suffering that it teaches sympathy or fellow-feeling. And sympathy breeds tolerance.

*   *   *

Jesus' fame as a healer had spread in this strange underworld of nomad patients. But they dare not approach too near him. The most pathetic feature in the narrative is that they had to waylay him and then call to him from a distance. All they got for their cries was a curt injunction to go to the priests and see if they could obtain a certificate of cure. It required a good deal of faith to fly in the face of probability and obey the command. But, as they did so, they found that the miracle had happened and that they were 'cleansed'.

One cannot help pausing a moment to reflect on our modern methods. The long-sustained faith of doctors and scientists has at last developed, if not a cure, at any rate a means of arresting the disease and making the patient no longer a danger to society. Nothing can restore lost limbs or tissue; but sufferers can be allowed back to their homes to live, as far as possible in the circumstances, a normal life. If only some means could be found of detecting the disease at the beginning of its uniquely long period of incubation, our devoted medical missionaries and researchers would be well on the way to eradicating it altogether.

*   *   *

Attention shifts to the one leper who, finding that he was healed, turned back to thank the giver of this unexpected bounty. It was of course the despised foreigner.

Courtesy comes where one least expects it. It seems to shine like an inner light in some natures without any effort to kindle it. It is a part of the disposition with which a favoured few seem to be born. The majority have to learn it by slow and painful effort, and in doing so to suffer humiliating lapses. But in either case it often catches the beholder by surprise, and brings the special pleasure of witnessing the work of unexpected grace.

Even when streamlined into a routine it illumines every part of the human scene. Whether it is in athletic sports like Judo and fencing, or in religious activities like those of priest and server at the altar, mutual courtesies are intended to reveal, and thereby increase and enhance, the spirit of the undertaking.

Etiquette can be exaggerated and formal, and can become a sheer weariness to all concerned, but at heart it is a reflection of the humble and grateful love of God and our fellow-men. It breathes the spirit of the Samaritan's thanks and of Mary's *Magnificat*. In Belloc's memorable words:

> *Of courtesy—it is much less*
> *Than courage of heart or holiness,*
> *Yet in my walks it seems to me*
> *That the Grace of God is in Courtesy.*

ANXIETY

Trinity XV   *St. Matthew* 6. 24

THERE is no doubt that one of the greatest troubles
of our time, perhaps the greatest, is anxiety. In spite
of the Welfare State and the material security it offers
from the cradle to the grave, we are still bothered about
our future, about our health, about the children, about a
thousand and one things that rob us of our peace of
mind.

In fact the more sophisticated we become the more we
suffer from this anxiety neurosis. In a primitive society,
so long as people are protected from physical danger
and have food and a covering, they may be content. But
our needs multiply the better off we are, and we are
always finding fresh wants to worry us.

There are indeed those, like the famous Dane, Kierkegaard, for whom life becomes too much. Not all have his
touch of genius to transmute their own anguish into a key
for the understanding of the human mind. Most sink
beneath their load and, at best, find their effectiveness
reduced. They live in a state of continued despondency.
Their friends think their misery is their own fault, and
they get very little of the human sympathy for which
they crave.

*   *   *

This trouble must have been already prevalent in
the confused state of society when Jesus lived among men.
Otherwise he would hardly have spent so much time in
warning his hearers against its dangers. No doubt the
exhortation we have in our Sunday's gospel is a collection
of short sayings uttered at different times. Even so the

total amount is impressive because it occupies more space than the gospels usually devote to one topic.

Jesus puts his finger at once upon the root cause of the disability. People are trying to serve two masters at the same time. 'You cannot serve God and Mammon.' Mammon is simply money personified. Here it stands for all selfish and material desires. We cannot divide our allegiance between God and ourselves.

How prevalent is this trouble today we can recognize from what we read of passing events in our newspapers. No doubt those who were guilty of the great train robbery and of a thousand and one other crimes of robbery with violence expect to be able to live as respectable members of society on the proceeds of their misdeeds. But the two kinds of life are totally incompatible, and whatever may be the outward appearance the strain on the whole inner personality is bound to reveal the effect of the cleavage.

* * *

Once we have admitted this basic fact and resolved to recognize God's prior claim on our lives, there ensues an immediate sense of freedom. We feel like the child who has been essaying an impossible task and then suddenly finds it taken out of his hands. So we realize that, so far from being able to run other people's lives, we cannot even run our own; and in the moment of realization we remember that we are all alike in God's hands, and in that knowledge we are content. We are prepared to leave everything to him—not that we are unwilling to do our share, but that we do all in future at his dictation.

The basic quality we need is trust. 'Such trust have we to Godward, not that we are sufficient to think anything of ourselves, but our sufficiency is of God.' What we cannot do for ourselves, he will do for us. We shall meet each day's worries as they come, recognizing that 'our times are in his hands, who said "A whole I planned".'

It is a new state of mind that we need. 'Seek ye first the Kingdom.' Let our one anxiety be to do God's will and we shall find that the rest falls into place. In that confidence we can face the future without fear. 'In his will is our peace', said Dante. Or we can remember Browning to the same effect: 'Trust God; see all; nor be afraid.' Or, better still, St. Peter: 'Casting all your care upon him, for he careth for you.'

COMPASSION

THE story of the miracle at Nain comes from St. Luke's special source. None of the other evangelists knows it or has used it. How wonderful that St. Luke should have preserved it and recorded it so beautifully.

It is very simply told. Jesus meets the funeral procession coming out of the village. He ignores the regulations against defilement, puts his hand on the bier and stops the procession. He then bids the dead man get up, and the youth sits up and begins talking, whereupon Jesus hands him over to his mother.

That is the gist of the story, but in telling it so we have not only mutilated it but given it a twist quite different from the evangelist's. We have hardly mentioned the mother, and it is upon her that St. Luke rivets attention; 'The only son of his mother, and she was a widow.' She was very much liked, for 'much people of the city was with her'. It was her tears that drew Jesus' compassion. 'Don't cry' was the first word he said. It was into her keeping that he delivered the restored youth.

The crowd was moved to awe and praise at the emergence of this great prophet, but there can be no doubt that the widow would think most of the tenderness of Jesus.

*   *   *

Those critics then cannot be wholly right who think that St. Luke's purpose in recording this miracle is to draw attention to the power of Jesus as a wonder-worker. One doubts whether any of the gospel records were written from quite that point of view. It is either taken for granted or recorded in the plaudits of the crowd.

No doubt it is part of the intention of the writer to make clear the Lord's power over life and death. Incidentally that rare use of the title 'Lord', rare at least so far as the gospels are concerned, helps to bring out the same point. He who can bring the dead to life is Lord indeed, of greater power than the Roman emperor who sat upon the throne of the world and claimed divinity; comparable even to the Lord of the scriptures who was none other than the High God, Jehovah.

Something of this the crowd already felt when they began to recognize Jesus as the expected Messiah, or at least the great prophet who was expected to usher in his appearance. But St. Luke's main purpose, while remaining faithful to his text, is to emphasize the human quality of Jesus, his tenderness to a widow woman, his reaction to her tears, his happiness in restoring her lost son.

*   *   *

It is surely on this level that we are intended to react to the story today. Domestic tragedies are common to the race. We all suffer under them: they are inevitable. And death is the commonest, for it comes to all alike. So essential a part is it of our human lot that some of our contemporary philosophers hold that we should make it the starting-point of all our thinking.

But to be perpetually looking into the abyss of annihilation or nothingness was very far from Jesus' teaching. He would rather make us feel that in the midst of death we are in life. It is no part of his task to change the physical character of human life, to banish from it all material decay and dissolution. That must wait for a new world in which a new set of conditions will prevail. But he can here and now in a particular situation relieve the agony of a bereaved parent and restore to each other a loved and loving mother and son.

L

So from one instance we must learn to know God's mind in all. It is the compassion of Jesus that brings us comfort in our trouble; his reflection of the love of a heavenly Father who did not exclude himself from the human predicament, but allowed his own Son to die the cruellest of deaths in order that he might lead us without fear of parting into total victory and everlasting peace.

TABLE TALK

AT first sight Sunday's gospel looks like an almost casual extract from some tradition of Jesus' table-talk. It may indeed be that St. Luke has set down two unrelated pieces of conversation so that their very contrast may illustrate the many-sidedness of our Lord's discourse. It would still be true that the two items, taken individually and understood quite superficially, throw a vivid light on Jesus' characteristic manner of teaching.

It is probable, however, that a little probing below the surface will show an underlying connection between them and reveal Christ's thoughts on the most profound of all questions, namely, how we get our salvation.

The scene is laid in the house of an important Pharisee by whom Jesus is being entertained to a meal on the Sabbath day. When a man suffering from dropsy appears, Jesus knows that his host's friends are watching him to see whether he will commit a technical breach of the holy day.

Instead of waiting to be questioned, Jesus takes the initiative, and asks them what they would do in the case of a domestic animal which had fallen into grievous danger on the Sabbath day. He knows quite well that they would regard themselves as exempt from the Sabbath regulation in their need to rescue so valuable a piece of property. Of course they would save it, Sabbath or not.

The retort that a human being is much more valuable than any beast and much more worth saving, even on the Sabbath, is so obvious that it does not need to be made. The meticulous quibbling over legalistic details is silenced in face of so clear an indication of the demands of charity.

We do not need to be told that Jesus was left to heal his patient; but we are told that he was able to continue his meal in peace.

*   *   *

It comes almost as a shock in the next item of conversation to find Jesus turning the tables and indulging in one of his rare flashes of humour. He had noticed with amusement, and perhaps contempt, the care with which some of the guests, in finding their places at table, had insisted on their rights of precedence, and had even tried surreptitiously to usurp a higher place than was their due.

If you really want to do yourselves some good, said Jesus in effect, I can tell you how to do it. Don't go and grab the best seats for yourselves: you will only be turned out and be thoroughly humiliated. What you should do is to go and sit down in a seat which is obviously below your rank and status. Then your host, when he sees you, can't possibly leave you there. He will have to ask you to move up higher.

Here again the story bears a lesson on its face. But in this case it is spelled out for us. 'Whosoever exalteth himself shall be abased; and he that humbleth himself shall be exalted.' The evangelist sees a serious purpose in the fun Jesus pokes at the vanity of his fellow-guests, and he does not mean us to miss the simple moral lesson.

*   *   *

The very fact that he has been at such pains to point the moral makes us ask whether he did not mean to impel his readers to look for something even more important than a lesson in table-manners. The answer is not far to seek.

In both items of conversation the underlying thought is not of any temporal benefit but of eternal salvation.

People are in danger of missing it for various reasons. Some are so full of scrupulosity about minor details that they may easily let fall the substance while grasping after the shadow. Others are so concerned about their standing in this world that they forget the importance of the life everlasting.

In both cases the mistake lies in thinking that they can get what they want for themselves. Neither healing nor assurance can come as the result of our own effort. The only possible means is a deep, root-and-branch, humility. We are nothing. God is all.

TRUE CHRISTIANITY

ANYONE trying to answer the question, 'What is Christianity?' from Sunday's gospel might be forgiven for thinking that it was best described as an ellipse with two foci, one concerned with right behaviour and the other with the Messiah. Certainly the passage falls naturally into those two divisions. But they are in such sharp contrast that they need to be understood and brought together.

The first section deals with our attitude towards life. What is the right standard to adopt? Love towards God and one's neighbour. That statement is in line with a number of passages of scripture which sum up in succinct terms the proper attitude of the good man. 'This is pure religion and undefiled, to visit the fatherless and widow in their affliction and to keep oneself unspotted from the world.' 'What does the Lord thy God require of thee but to do justice and to love mercy and to walk before God all the days of thy life?'

It is well that we should bear these summaries in mind. They put the rules for our behaviour in a nutshell and they give us something to fall back upon when we are in doubt.

*   *   *

The second half of the gospel deals with a very different matter. Admittedly it is a piece of debate, an argument with some critics who were trying to catch Jesus out and whom he was answering in their own language. 'From whose line is the Messiah to descend?' From that of David, the king who was the very type of the Messiah. But, in a country where veneration for parents was one of the foundations of society, no father could rank his children above himself. 'How then', says Jesus, 'can David call the Messiah his Lord?'

No doubt the psalm from which the quotation is taken was originally a coronation anthem describing the divine favour bestowed upon the monarch now ascending to his throne. 'God says to our King, "Sit at my right hand while I put your enemies under your feet."' But its significance had been lifted a stage higher to apply to the Messiah, and Jesus, accepting the common notion that David was the author, suggests that it is illogical for the founder of a dynasty to hail his successor as greater than himself. The Messiah cannot be David's son and his master at the same time.

Those early Christians who first heard the story knew the solution of the riddle. Jesus, who put the question, was himself the Messiah, and included in himself the attributes both of humility and royalty. He was indeed the descendant of David; he had been born in a carpenter's dwelling; and yet he was destined to sit at the right hand of God and to rule not only Israel but the world.

* * *

How now are we to reconcile these two contrasting interests: right behaviour and the descent of the Messiah?

We too, like the early Christians, must see the answer in the life and character of Jesus. He is our Lord, and it is he who bids us love God and our neighbours. We know how exceedingly difficult this apparently simple commandment is to fulfil. Left to ourselves, we soon find our love of God and our desire to help others grow cold. We have no energy of ourselves, and we must keep as close as possible to him in order to draw from him strength to meet our weakness.

Jesus himself shows us how close that relationship may be. 'I am the vine, ye are the branches. As the branch cannot bear fruit of itself, so neither can ye except ye abide in me.'

The charge to love God and one's neighbour will become possible to obey when the life of Messiah expresses itself in us, when 'it is no longer I that live but Christ that liveth in me'. There is really only one short answer to the question 'What is Christianity'? The answer is 'Christianity is incorporation into Christ.'

SIN AND DISEASE

THE Gospel for Sunday is a typical section or 'form' of
the evangelical narrative. It is a concise little story
with its precise point set in its concluding words. No doubt
it had been told over and over again and became stereotyped long before it was included in any written account
of our Lord's life.

It records an encounter between Jesus and the Scribes,
and may indeed have been the first such encounter in the
long series of clashes that led finally to his death. We should
remember that the Scribes were not just writers or secre-
taries. They were the expounders of the Law, the section
of society to which the title Rabbi was later confined.

The clash came over a question of healing. A paralytic
had been brought to Jesus; and Jesus, recognizing the
faith of those who had brought him, and no doubt seeing
the man's real need, told him at once, 'Your sins are
forgiven.'

To the Scribes such a statement seemed sheer blasphemy. It meant that a mere man was arrogating to
himself the prerogative of God. And according to the
Mosaic Law anyone perpetrating such a crime was worthy
of the supreme penalty.

*   *   *

Why had Jesus addressed himself to the man's moral
condition instead of taking the more obvious course and
dealing straightway with his medical need? Perhaps
because he wished to make it clear that his healings were
not merely physical cures but were intended as a sign
that the Kingdom of God had come. In that Kingdom

righteousness was of more importance than physical health. Salvation meant wholeness; and in a perfect existence the well-being of soul and body must go together.

The question of the association between morality and health has always been in debate. There are some illnesses that are the obvious results of evil living; and this man's paralysis may well have been of that kind. If that is so, Jesus showed great insight in speaking first of his sins.

Jesus himself was careful at another time to point out the folly of *always* associating disease with sin. That the connection does sometimes exist is nevertheless well known, and the knowledge of the fact has been widely recognized today in our study of psychosomatic diseases. Jesus was following what is now well established medical practice by ensuring that his patient's mind was at ease before he set in action the physical cure. To this aspect of the case the Scribes were blinded by their religious and theological prejudices.

*   *   *

We get near to the heart of the narrative when we consider our Lord's reply to their charge. He will let them know that the Son of Man has power on earth to forgive sins. This is no blasphemy but the exercise of a divinely bestowed prerogative.

Who is this Son of Man? The Messiah, no doubt. But scholars have told us that the phrase has wider overtones. Sometimes Jesus uses it as if it were equivalent to the first person pronoun 'I'. At other times it seems to be better explained as pointing to the 'representative man'.

It seems as if both meanings are present here. Jesus is asserting that he himself has this power but he is also emphasizing the fact that human beings have some share in it. That is why the story ends as it does, with the crowd marvelling.

How much happier we might all be if we recognized the reconciling power in the community of Christian fellowship. When the Celtic monks went on their long and lonely journeys they were accustomed to take with them a 'soul-fellow' to whom they could confess their sins, as St. James had taught, and find forgiveness. The Church has provided us with ministers to serve the same purpose for us on our journey through life.

Many physical diseases are caused by the mental strain involved in too much reticence and personal isolation. To hear the word of pardon pronounced even by human lips is often the best way to physical recovery.

THE WEDDING GARMENT

THE parable of the marriage feast can be interpreted on two levels, that on which Jesus told it, and that on which St. Matthew recounted it. On the former level it has one main lesson—the call to enjoy a freely bestowed happiness in the Kingdom of Heaven.

In the beginning of all things, God had intended life on this planet to be a physical and spiritual paradise, a Garden of Eden and fellowship with himself in perpetuity. By his wilfulness man destroyed the fellowship and consequently the physical paradise was also spoilt. The Garden of Eden was exchanged for a hard and burdensome school, in which man could be disciplined and acquire the character that would make possible the renewal of fellowship with God.

At the turning-point of human history, Jesus came announcing the restoration of that fellowship in himself. Those who accepted his call entered into the new paradise, the Kingdom of God, where the primal joy of union with the Father could be recaptured, and where in due course the external environment would again match the inward bliss. Jesus addressed that call in the first instance to his own people, the Jews, and particularly to their religious leaders. They refused it with indifference amounting to contempt and issuing in ultimate violence. Jesus now turned to the people of no account, those who had no obvious claim upon him, and offered them the same happiness on the same generous terms. The parable is his challenge to the multitude.

*   *   *

As St. Matthew told the story, and as his congregation heard it read, the interpretation would inevitably take on fresh overtones of meaning from contemporary conditions. Jesus himself had not only been rejected but crucified. His Resurrection and Ascension had brought no change in the temper of the Jewish people. The few who had accepted him as Messiah had started the Church on its long history. The Church had repeated Jesus' appeal to the Jews and had been rejected like its Master. It had turned to the Gentiles, but although it had more success there, the Roman Government had decided against it, and there had been bitter persecution. Jerusalem itself had been destroyed. Hitherto the bulk of the Christians had escaped, but some of the leaders had already lost their lives.

Rejected by Jew and Roman alike, the Church found its most numerous converts among the less significant masses. To them happiness was freely offered. The slaves, the little men, the outcasts, the smaller tradesmen, of whom the congregation was largely composed, had themselves responded to this gracious invitation. They had found life transformed, their fears removed, their troubles relieved, and themselves seated with Christ at the perpetual banquet of new and unalloyed happiness. Such has been Christian experience ever since.

*   *   *

The appendix to the story, describing the man who would not put on the wedding gown freely provided for the guests, emphasizes the churlishness with which Christ's gifts are rejected, and the punishment such rejection deserves. If it seems almost incredible that anyone coming to the feast should refuse this small courtesy, let us reflect how often we ourselves refuse, with little or no reason, to be happy.

For St. Matthew's immediate circle of readers the lesson

would be that the Church on earth was not co-terminous with the saved. In the congregation, saints and sinners were intermingled. Some might even share in the breaking of bread who were not wholly committed to Christ and his way.

For us the lesson is that even among Christians there are some who will not put on the garment of Christian joy. They will not remember that life is intended to be a feast. 'The world's so full of a number of things. . . .' 'If I have faltered more or less in my great task of happiness. . . .' 'And make thy chosen people joyful.' 'That your joy may be full.' The familiar phrases leap to the mind. If Jesus invites us to a wedding, why should we persist in wearing 'the garment of heaviness'?

FAITH AND THE SIGN

Trinity XXI   *St. John* 4. 46

'THIS is the second sign that Jesus did.' A wonderful
work, certainly, this healing of the nobleman's son.
But a sign of what?

A sign is an indication of something that is not immediately obvious. A sign-post is a pointer to a town or
village that is still in the distance. This miracle then is
intended to hint at some underlying truth which is not
clearly indicated on the surface.

Scholars in the past have shown a good deal of ingenuity
in trying to decide for us the precise truth to which the
miracles were intended to point. Today they appear to
have come to the conclusion that they were intended to be
signs of the Kingdom. Just as most of Jesus' parables were
stories told to illustrate the nature of God's rule on earth,
so the miracles were intended to give further enlighten-
ment of its character by means of occurrences in the
actual practice of daily life.

One point in particular the miracles were intended to
enforce. That was that the Kingdom was actually there.
It no longer lay wholly in the future. It was no longer
merely 'at hand'. It was there now in the midst of that
very generation of Jewish people. Its presence was being
made obvious by those wonderful works. Believers must
make haste to get into it.

*   *   *

It was not that the miracles were intended to 'compel'
people to believe in the Kingdom. It is obvious that in
the present instance the nobleman already had belief of a
sort: otherwise he would not have come to the Master.

When Jesus taxed him with waiting to see a 'wonder' in order to be convinced, he thrust the suggestion aside, anxious to get the one important business done and his son healed.

His very impatience showed faith sufficient for the healing. When afterwards he found by careful enquiry that the cure was effected at the very moment that Jesus had announced it, he felt assured that this could have been no mere coincidence and his faith was confirmed. 'Himself believed, and his whole house.'

In other words, he had to make the same choice that we all have to make when we are considering the great events in our own lives. Do we think that they all happened just by chance, that they were all the result of mere fortuitous circumstance? Or do we recognize in them the hand of God, arranging cause and effect until they have issued in the situation of the present moment? Either solution may be possible, but if we deliberately accept the second, we shall be 'lost in wonder, love, and praise'.

*   *   *

If we are accustomed to think in this way, we shall find it easy to realize that the age of miracles is not past. God still 'moves in a mysterious way his wonders to perform'. Our belief in his guidance and protection is continually being reinforced by some signal exhibition of his grace and kindness.

Indeed he has not left himself without a constant witness of his presence and activity. In our generation his sacraments are still the continuators of his miracles, the signs that his Kingdom is here.

Of course, we can give all sorts of other explanations. We can say that they are purely natural, the kind of visual aid that we are constantly producing for our children.

But we have been taught to think of them as *effective* signs, that is, signs that actually convey the gift they signify. Baptism really does mean a new life in Christ; Confirmation a real inspiration of the Holy Spirit; Holy Communion a real partaking of his personality; Absolution a real putting away of sin.

To accept this we need the same kind of preliminary faith shown by the nobleman. By it we can discern the spiritual meaning of the signs. In the resultant experience our belief is confirmed and we find ourselves at one with all the Christian ages, living in the Kingdom and enjoying all the miraculous gifts of the King.

M

UNFORGIVING SERVANT

*N*OBLESSE *OBLIGE*. The children of the Kingdom must display the manners of the Kingdom.

They are under obligation. 'Freely ye have received, freely give.' The parables of Jesus are almost universally intended to illustrate the nature of the Messianic Kingdom, and perhaps there is none that goes as deep into the heart of the matter as this. For this deals with the character of the citizens, and that at a fundamental point. For them, as the Frenchman said of God himself, forgiveness must be their *métier*.

It is not to be supposed that such a habit of mind can come easily or naturally. Our normal reaction to a wrong done is a feeling of resentment, followed quickly by a desire to exact retribution. This is not the law of the jungle only; it is the law of the nursery.

*   *   *

What then is the force that can penetrate deep down below the springs of action and change such feelings at the start? What indeed but the profound consciousness that we ourselves have been forgiven. If we realize that one against whom we have seriously offended has felt no resentment against us, but in spite of every provocation has done everything possible to bring about our lasting good and lead us into perfection, then it is almost impossible both to feel this deeply and at the same time to harbour hatred of another.

The difficulty is to feel adequately that we ourselves have been forgiven. The unforgiving servant must surely have forgotten, or put away from him, the thought of the debt that had been remitted in his own case. Even the sight of the crucifix and the memory of all that it implies may scarcely be sufficient to stab us broad awake. Here the influence of the redeemed community and our regular habit of confession may make us savingly aware of our own condition.

*   *   *

It will help us, too, to understand the full significance of the forgiving spirit. This is no negative quality, not a mere turning away from the offending person with the single purpose of forgetting. It is a creative impulse, anxious to restore the offender, and always watching for an opportunity to bring about complete reconciliation.

Nor is it just a once-for-all action, desiring to have done with an unpleasant situation. It is not the attitude of mind that can count the number of times such a benefit has been conferred. 'Not seven times, but seventy times seven.' The numbers imply wholeness, completeness. What is required is a fresh set of the whole personality, not occasional or spasmodic generosity, but a permanent determination always to serve the best and highest interests of all others, even those who have offended us most grievously. This is the main characteristic of the Kingdom, and the proper attitude of the whole family of God. How often do we hear of criminals defending themselves on the ground that 'society owes me something'. It is a perverse use of a legitimate plea. In a perfect community we should recognize the value of the aphorism 'all for each'.

The emergence of the Welfare State is an explicit admission of its truth. But a secular society can never remain long on the crest of the wave even of its own idealism. It has worked too long by force and law and repression. And so long as society remains imperfect, these means of restraint must inevitably be kept in use. All the more necessary, therefore, is it for the Church to act, as Jesus said, as the leaven to leaven the whole lump.

*   *   *

The pattern of the Kingdom must always be displayed before the eyes of the whole world. Within the divine family, mutual obligation is fully recognized, the debt owed by society to the individual and by the individual to society. Even more important is the recognition that this accommodation can never be satisfactorily attained on the basis of rule and regulation. It must be the outcome of the love that flows from the consciousness of sin forgiven. To that forgiveness we are traitors if we *from our hearts* forgive not every one his brother their trespasses.

DOUBLE LOYALTY

Trinity XXIII (Remembrance Day)   *St. Matthew* 22. 15

IT is good that on Remembrance Sunday we should
have for our gospel the story of the tribute money. Its
sharp reminder of our double duty, to God and Cæsar,
sets the sacrifice of those whom we commemorate in its
right perspective.

They may not be martyrs in the sense of those who die
for their faith, but they are heroes inasmuch as they died
in the performance of their duty. And who will say that
the one sacrifice is not as precious in God's sight as the
other?

*   *   *

It was an unholy alliance of patriots and collaborators
that approached Jesus with their question, 'Is it lawful
to give tribute to Cæsar?' They thought that whatever
answer he gave he would embroil himself either with the
nationalists or with the government. They must have been
surprised at the readiness with which he parried their
question, using the 'visual aid' of the actual coin in which
the tax was paid. It was stamped with the head of the
reigning Cæsar. By a commonly recognized convention,
the taxes were regarded as the property of the government that issued the current coinage. There could be no
question therefore: the money should go to the authority
that issued it. Their own Temple tax was paid in different
coinage, or perhaps in different denomination.

God and Cæsar were thus symbolized in contrasting
pieces of money. The normal citizen would use each coin
for its intended purpose.

*   *   *

The State then can make just demands of the Christian man. It is part of our religion to meet those demands as adequately as we can. St. Paul puts prayers for those in authority high in the list of civic virtues and he encourages obedience to the powers that be. St. Peter is most anxious that the people to whom he writes should do everything possible to show themselves good citizens and to attract no adverse notice either from their neighbours or from the authorities. St. Augustine recognizes that although the city of this world is very different from the City of God, nevertheless in so far as it maintains peace and order it is worthy of the Christian's respect and service.

The fact is that we cannot contract out of our civic obligations. Even the monk and the hermit are still citizens and serve the public well-being by their prayers and by their example. Nor is there any logical reason why we should try to avoid our obligations. The fact that we may not agree with all the State does is no excuse. Our Lord made his pronouncement in the reign of Tiberius, whom many regarded as a monster of iniquity. St. Peter was probably writing in the reign of Nero, who burnt Christians as human torches. Yet both are emphatic about the Christian's duty to serve the State.

*   *   *

The fact is that the State is an extension of the family. Not all the heads of families are good, yet the family as an institution gives us protection and maintenance during our infancy, and still in many ways serves our best interests even after we are able to care for ourselves. The State exercises the same care for its citizens in general. In these days of the Welfare State, the range of its interests has been extended to an enormous degree. All the more right has it to make demands of us in return.

Jesus does not here consider the question what is to

happen when the claims of God and Cæsar clash, but we know that both he and his immediate followers were prepared in such circumstances to go to their death rather than betray their primary allegiance to God. Those whom we commemorate on Remembrance Sunday were fortunate in that there appeared to them no clash between the earthly and heavenly powers. They saw their duty plain before them, and in the performance of it they lost their lives. It is the result of their devotion and sacrifice that we enjoy the benefits of freedom and independence today. Let us thank God and pray that we may prove worthy of what they have won for us.

NEW VITALITY

Trinity XXIV   *St. Matthew* 9. 18

OUR Prayer Book inserts the first line of Sunday's
gospel into the Biblical text in order to remind us
of the context in which St. Matthew, unlike the other two
synoptists, has placed the healing of the ruler's daughter
and of the woman with the issue of blood.

That context is Jesus' conversation with the disciples
of John the Baptist. They had begun with a question
about fasting, and Jesus had tried to enlarge their vision
and to make them realize that his mission was not intended
to deal with legal niceties, but to introduce a new era and
a new life. This would involve on their part a complete
reorientation. New wine must be put into new wine-
skins.

St. Matthew, recounting the story of that conversation,
seizes the opportunity to illustrate the character of the
new life in the Kingdom by introducing here two typical
miracles. Jesus' days are so full that even on the way to
perform one act of compassion he is called upon to perform another. He is surrounded by such crowds that it
seems absurd to ask who touched him. His own vitality
is so abounding that it overflows to heal and bless all
who come to him in faith. It is a picture of such a happy,
busy existence as could not fail to attract the sympathetic
attention of the congregation for whom St. Matthew
writes.

*   *   *

The woman to whom relief was so unexpectedly given
was an example of severely handicapped people. Her particular ailment made her ceremonially unclean according

to Jewish law. She could not approach Jesus openly, but came up behind him unseen, and just touched the fringe or tassel of his outer garment. She believed that there was magic power in his body, and that a mere touch of his clothing would set it in action. Such faith was more than half superstition. Yet it was faith of a kind, the only kind probably of which up to that moment she was capable; and Jesus responded immediately even to so immature an approach.

Eusebius, writing early in the fourth century, tells us that he saw a statue in Cæsarea Philippi of this woman 'at the gates of her house, on an elevated stone . . . on her bended knee, with her hands stretched out before her like one entreating.' Whether the identification is accurate or not, it is evidence of the importance the early Church attached to the incident. It revealed the beginning of the new age, an age in which all the old regulations and taboos had either disappeared or been reduced to a very secondary place. A new vitality had come into existence. Of it those who were in touch with Christ were privileged to be the partakers.

*   *   *

The lesson is driven home in the raising of the ruler's daughter. Whether she had just died and was really dead, as her father and the neighbours thought, or whether she was merely in a state of unconsciousness, which they in their haste and confusion had taken for death, as Jesus seems to suggest, does not matter. The inference in either case is that in the new age a fresh attitude to the grave is warranted for Christians. Death is no longer the end of life. We are no longer under the dominance of a blind inexorable fate. In the eyes of God and of Jesus death itself is no more than a sleep.

St. Matthew's readers, who looked back on this incident

from the vantage point of the post-Resurrection appearances of Christ, would recognize it as another instance of the way in which death had been made the gate of a new life. No doubt mourning customs still lingered, and pagan or Jewish neighbours would still laugh Christian pretensions to scorn. But they themselves knew that they had passed from death into life. They had each become the fount of a new creative energy. They were each possessed of a new moral force. They were actually living within the Kingdom. They must so yield to their new environment that their conduct, their words, even their thoughts would become redolent of its fragrance.

It is still within that new vitality that we live and move and have our being today.

HEAVENLY FOOD

IT has often been asked why the evangelists or their
predecessors arranged the fragmentary stories about
our Lord's life and teaching, which they had received
from the oral tradition, in their present context. Sometimes, no doubt, they believed they were following the
chronological order; at others they no less certainly
arranged their material according to its subject-matter.

The author of the fourth Gospel had his own highly
individual method of treatment. He liked to take a particular feast, tell the story of some miracle that occurred at
it, and then recount a homily that brings out the teaching
both of the feast and the miracle and relates it to the
practical realities of the Christian life.

Thus in this great sixth chapter of St. John we get first
the mention of the Passover, at which, of course, a meal
formed the main part of the ceremonies. Then we get
the story of the meal in the desert, the miraculous feeding
of the five thousand. And then, after a short interlude,
during which Jesus and his followers pass to the other side
of the lake, we have the long and most moving discourse
on the heavenly manna, the true bread from heaven, by
eating of which we may expect to partake of eternal life.

*   *   *

The association with the Passover is important, because
that was the occasion of the great national deliverance
when the chosen people were rescued from threatened
destruction. It was thus the guarantee of entry into the
promised land, and of sharing in the future Messianic
feast. The miracle of the loaves gives a new turn to these

age-old thoughts. It shows that the Kingdom has already arrived, ushered in by a Messiah who can feed his people abundantly even in the wilderness. It also looks to the future and offers a pledge of final deliverance from man's last enemy and a share in the joys of heaven.

This account was no doubt intended to be read as a lesson at meetings of the congregation. The hearers would realize how many of the details fitted into the service upon which they were engaged. The boy with his loaves and fishes would remind them of the young men bringing the offertory of bread and wine. The four actions of Jesus in first taking, then blessing ('eucharist' giving thanks), thirdly breaking (v. 12, 'broken pieces'), and finally distributing, were precisely the actions of the celebrant at their own holy table, as they have been on similar occasions ever since. Even the term used for the gathering of the fragments, synaxis, was the technical name for the weekly gathering of the whole family of the local church. The congregation would be well prepared for the homily on the meaning of the Eucharist which was to follow.

*   *   *

In that homily St. John shows in his usual fashion how closely related are material and spiritual realities. Just as he has himself insisted on the material miracle in connection with the loaves and fishes and yet brought out in every detail its spiritual significance, so he shows how Jesus used the most materialistic language about eating his flesh and blood, and yet at the same time affirmed that only 'he that believeth hath eternal life'. The close affinity between material and spiritual is emphasized also in the analogy of the manna. The fathers who ate the manna in the wilderness died in spite of it because it had no spiritual content. But Jesus is the true manna, the bread of life, the bread that has the principle of life in itself. Those who feed on him share in this life-principle and therefore cannot die eternally.

The miracle of the feeding thus points forward to a more satisfying food than that which was given in the wilderness. It adumbrates the feast in which we assimilate the very personality of Christ himself. That food is super-abundant: there is plenty left over when everyone has had his fill. But due economy must be observed. There must be no waste, but each as he is able must make full use of the food supplied. It is not intended to satisfy idle curiosity or a desire for wonders, but to strengthen us for the journey and battle of life. Above all, it demands that we, having received the heavenly food ourselves, should henceforth continually 'strengthen the brethren'.

By the same author:

Reflections on the Collects
Reflections on the Epistles
The Four Great Heresies
What the Church of England stands for
The minds behind the new Theology